Broken Places

A MEMOIR

NANCY WHITFIELD

For Rick and our daughter, Kathryn

"The world breaks everyone and afterward many are strong at the broken places."

—Ernest Hemingway

PROLOGUE
HER MAJESTY, QUEEN SILVIA

Trapped in the backseat of a yellow cab on Central Park South, tense and sweating in our formal evening wear, we alternated between checking the time, craning our necks, and praying for the gridlock in front of us to disappear. Traffic in New York always conspired against us when we needed to get somewhere in a hurry, and tonight was no exception.

Our cab was inching towards the Harvard Club, one of the city's premiere private social enclaves. With a venerable history stretching back to 1887 and an illustrious membership including world leaders, cultural icons and more than a few billionaires, it is the pinnacle of refinement and a guardian of revered traditions.

On this particular evening, the club was playing host to the World Childhood Foundation's annual fundraising gala. Presiding over the affair was no less a luminary than Her Majesty, Queen Silvia of Sweden. My husband, Rick, and I would receive an introduction to the Queen, if our taxi ever made it across town.

Rick sprang the invitation on me the day before as we both engaged in another inescapable hallmark of Manhattan living: the morning battle for bathroom space.

I was standing at the sink, wiping the fog from the mirror and making my third attempt to apply mascara, when he shouted above the noise of the shower, "Nancy, we've been invited to a black-tie benefit at the Harvard Club tomorrow night. Do you want to go?"

The invitation came from the law firm Nixon Peabody. Rick worked closely with senior management from several Wall Street firms and often joined them at after-hours functions.

Like many of the invitations we received, this one was last minute and lacking in detail. The implication was obvious: rather than face the prospect of empty seats around the table, Nixon Peabody turned to its "B list." My husband's boyish good looks, charm, and impeccable Southern manners made him an ideal choice. The fine wine and food we enjoyed at these events more than compensated us for our lack of status.

Some women would panic over such short notice to an elegant affair but not me. I'm low-maintenance and have my routine down to three simple steps. Manicure/pedicure on my lunch hour, swap out my usual neutral lipstick for Revlon's *Cherries in the Snow,* and hop into my go-to formal ensemble: a black sequin top and silk slacks. Like a military uniform, it hung in my closet carefully veiled in its dry-cleaning bag, ready for the call of duty at a moment's notice. It's effortless, always appropriate and has served me well on numerous occasions. However, as our taxi screeched to a halt at 35 East 44th Street, my first thought was, *but maybe not this time.*

Paparazzi, each straining to gain an advantage over the other, flanked the entrance to the Club. Flashbulbs exploded as limo doors opened and women in designer ball gowns stepped onto the red carpet leading up the steps of the building. We managed to arrive with just moments to spare, but as I looked down at my dated sequin top and silk slacks, I wanted to hide. Rick, as if reading my thoughts, sprang from the cab and offered me his hand.

"We mustn't keep the Queen waiting."

I looked at the grin that won my heart years ago and couldn't resist smiling. My mother was right when she said I would never regret marrying my best friend. I took his arm, and together we strolled down the red carpet and crossed the threshold of the club.

Faster than I could say "John Harvard," a glass of champagne appeared in my hand, and someone escorted us to the reception hall. Moments later, a pronounced hush fell over the crowd, and all eyes turned toward the door. Her Majesty, Queen Silvia, entered the room and faced her audience with dignity that gave new meaning to the word *royalty*. Her striking red gown made it impossible to imagine she possessed anything short of immense confidence. Following behind the Queen, her daughter, Princess Madeleine, appeared in a strapless cobalt blue dress with tiny crystals sprinkled across the entire creation.

Rick, mesmerized by the two visions of loveliness standing before him, stood with a glass of champagne poised inches from his open mouth. I glanced down at my old sequin top and silk trousers and couldn't wait to be seated.

A receiving line formed as the Queen and her entourage prepared to welcome their guests. My mind started racing. What was the protocol? Should I introduce myself, shake hands or bow? It was too late to ask. The next moment I found myself looking into the eyes of the Queen.

"I hope your time in New York will be most enjoyable," I said, holding her hand in mine.

I surprised myself. I didn't say anything I would later regret or anguish over for days. Rick embraced Princess Madeleine's slender hand, but since I tend to be even more critical of his social judgement than my own, I avoided listening to his remarks. Whatever he said didn't matter. I turned and left him to bask in the glow of Madeline.

As the melodic voice of Peter Joback, a popular Swedish singer/songwriter, echoed through the club, a small bell summoned everyone to the dining hall. Since moving to Manhattan, I had grown accustomed to unique experiences such as this, yet I was still surprised to find myself a part of them. One minute I might be pushing my way through a turnstile in a grimy subway and the next, dining with the Queen of Sweden. In New York, anything was possible.

The rich mahogany paneling of Harvard Hall, matched the refined elegance of the evening's event. I sat down and immediately slid the imitation Gucci evening clutch I purchased on Canal Street under my chair. In this setting, it practically screamed *imposter.*

Waiters moved flawlessly among tables as they served filet mignon with béarnaise sauce and filled wine glasses. I glanced across the room and observed Queen Silvia speaking with the guests at her table. I admired her effortless sophistication. In truth, I envied it. Like most small towns in the South, the one in which I grew up offered scant opportunity to acquire cultural knowledge, much less hone one's social skills. Even after six years in Manhattan, I had yet to master the fundamentals of good taste.

The conversation around my table was lively, but I found it difficult to concentrate. Memories of my first trip to New York came rushing back. I was a seventeen-year-old girl who dreamed of escaping from small-town life and ways.

Memories of another trip also flooded my mind, those of a journey that marked the beginning of a lifetime of family secrets and half-veiled truths. I can still picture the station and Johnny in my mother's arms.

KANSAS CITY 1

"Hurry girls! We should already be in our seats."

A quick glance over her shoulder assured my mother we were nearby, so she continued to press through the crowd and make her way toward the train. She held my two-year-old brother, Johnny, in one arm and a large bag hung on the other.

Our journey began in the early morning hours when we caught a bus from our hometown of Clarksville, Tennessee, to Union Station in Nashville. I was eager to begin the adventure my mother had described with such flourish, but my expectations were shattered the moment we boarded the bus. It was drab, dirty and had an odor that made me want to hold my breath. I crawled in the seat behind my sister, Linda, just as the sun broke across the sky.

Warm air blew from a small heater anchored above the driver, but it didn't reach our seats. I was cold, and as we jostled down Highway 31, I snuggled closer to my mother and her fur coat. Two balls of fur dangled from her collar, and I reached up and smacked them.

"Stop. You'll wake Johnny," she said.

Johnny, Johnny, Johnny. Everything was about Johnny. He was asleep in her lap and had full advantage of the coat's warmth. I wanted to pinch his cheek, but instead I turned and drew figures on the frosty window beside me.

We arrived at Union Station ahead of schedule, but seconds before we heard our boarding call, Johnny got sick. My mother rushed him to the bathroom, and now we were about to miss the train.

I tried to keep up, but at four, I was no match for my heavy suitcase. I glanced at Linda and saw that despite being six, she wasn't faring any better than I was. Through sheer determination, we managed to drag our luggage across the platform and turn it over to the porter. My mother stood waiting by the steps of the first car. She looked tired and kept shifting Johnny from one arm to the other. The heavy bag hanging from her shoulder appeared to weigh even more than he did.

"You folks better hurry on board. This train is about to leave," the porter said.

We climbed the steps and followed our mother to the rear of the car. Just as we sat down, steam began surging from beneath the train, and we started to move. I stared out the window and watched Nashville slowly disappear. At last, we were on our way to Kansas City.

The porter came down the aisle, and my mother handed him our tickets.

"I'll stop by later with some pillows and blankets for the children. There's food in the dining car if anyone gets hungry."

The words *dining car* stuck in my mind.

"Are we going to eat in the dining car?" I asked.

"No, it's too expensive. I packed some snacks for later."

Snacks from my mother's handbag lacked the appeal of eating in the dining car, but I knew better than to ask again. Whenever she used the term *too expensive,* it always signaled the end of the conversation.

The train gathered speed and swayed back and forth along the track. Somewhere between Nashville and St. Louis, I fell asleep. When I woke, Linda and Johnny were asleep, and my mother was arranging blankets around them. My stomach growled and thoughts of the dining car resurfaced.

"I'm hungry," I said.

"I'll get out the snacks," whispered my mother.

At the mention of food, my sister and brother sat up at full attention.

"Is Daddy in Kansas City?" I asked after finishing my snack.

"Yes."

"Why?"

"I've already told you. He's visiting his family. You should get some more sleep. You've been up since early this morning."

My parents produced three off springs in five years, but unfortunately, other parts of their marriage were not as fruitful. By the time I was three, their marriage was crumbling and my father was rarely at home. Contrary to what my mother told us, he wasn't visiting his family. He had abandoned us. I had gotten used to his absence, so it never occurred to me anything might be amiss.

My parents met in the right place but at the wrong time. Battles were raging in Europe, and the United States had officially entered World War II. Like most patriotic young Americans, my father wanted to serve his country, so he said goodbye to his home in Kansas City and enlisted in the army.

A few weeks later, he reported to Fort Campbell, a military base located just outside of Clarksville, the town where my mother lived. She was a gifted pianist and devoted much of her time to performing, but she dreamed of marriage and raising a family. It was a predictable path for women of her generation.

One Sunday, feeling isolated and downhearted, my father drove to town seeking encouragement and companionship. He found both when he stumbled into the local Methodist Church. When the service ended, he received an invitation to lunch from my mother's parents. During the War, they frequently extended this offer to young soldiers, most of whom were away from home for the first time.

My father's striking appearance and good manners did not escape my mother's notice, nor did her charm and talent elude his. In spite of their short relationship, when my father received orders to report to Europe, they married. My mother spent the next two years waiting out the war and writing letters to my father. When the war ended, he returned to Clarksville.

Our trip to Kansas City was a desperate attempt to rescue my parents' marriage. My mother was hopeful we would ignite my father's paternal feelings and bring him home. In other words, we were her bait.

It was late when we reached Kansas City, and we took a cab to my grandparents' house. When the door opened, the expression on my grandmother's face made it clear she was surprised to see us.

"I've brought the children to see their father," my mother said quickly.

"Is he aware of this?"

"No, but I'm sure he'll be glad we've come."

"I hope for your sake that's true. I'll call and let him know you and the children are here."

Where was Daddy? We waited in the hall while my grandmother phoned. My grandfather looked from one of us to the other but he didn't speak. Johnny fell asleep, and my mother carried him to the couch in the living room. When my grandmother returned, she said Daddy wasn't coming.

"I assume you've made plans to stay somewhere tonight. Jim wasn't pleased when I told him you were here, and I won't get involved in your problems."

A tear fell from my mother's eye and disappeared halfway down her face.

"I don't expect you to get involved, but Jim is a grown man with a wife and three children. He's involved whether he wants to be or not. Please, Leona, we have to stay here. We have nowhere else to go."

"You should have thought of that before dragging these children all the way to Kansas City. It was irresponsible."

"Irresponsible? What do you call deserting a wife and three children?"

My grandfather spoke up and said if we left first thing in the morning, that we could spend the night at their house. I didn't want to stay, but no one asked.

I followed my grandmother to a bedroom at the end of the hall. She removed a blanket from the closet and laid it at the foot of the bed. After turning the covers back, she asked if I needed help getting ready for bed. Did she think I was a baby?

"I can get ready by myself."

"Then I'll say goodnight, so you can get some sleep."

Before she reached the door, she stopped and turned.

"I know this is hard, but one day you'll understand."

She closed the door, and I listened to her footsteps going down the hall. As soon as it was quiet, I undressed and crawled in bed. I wished we had never come to Kansas City. I wanted to go home. Where was my mother? When was Daddy coming? I went to sleep without answers.

The house was quiet the next morning, and I lay in bed thinking about the previous night. It wasn't long before my mother came to fix my hair.

"Are we going home today?"

"Yes, we're leaving right after breakfast."

"Are we going to see Daddy?"

"No, not this time. Hold still while I tie this ribbon."

I searched her face for answers but found none. Over time, I learned to accept her silence as an appropriate response to things I didn't understand.

"When you finish dressing, come to the kitchen. Breakfast is on the table."

Why couldn't we see Daddy? We had come so far to see him. I finished dressing, stuffed my pajamas in my bag and went to the kitchen.

"Sit next to your sister," my mother said.

I walked around the table and pulled out a chair next to Linda. My grandmother's eyes never left the skillet in front of her. My grandfather was sitting at the end of the table. The newspaper in his hands rustled when he turned the pages, but he didn't speak. No one spoke, and the silence frightened me. Something must have happened – something so terrible no one could talk about it.

As soon as we finished breakfast, my grandfather put our luggage in the trunk of his car and drove us back to the station. When we arrived, he unloaded our bags and kissed each of us goodbye. I glanced at my mother and saw tears in her eyes.

"Wave goodbye to your grandfather," she said as his car pulled away from the curb. We waved goodbye, gathered our belongings and went inside to wait for the train.

I never saw my grandparents again, and no one ever mentioned our trip to Kansas City. Vague and unpleasant memories of it haunted me for years. It was the beginning of a lifetime of secrecy surrounding my father's disappearance.

UNINTENDED CONSEQUENCES   2

Our trip to Kansas City wasn't my mother's first attempt at reconciling with my father by preying on his paternal instincts. A prior attempt failed miserably. I know because I was part of that scheme, and although the damage was unintentional, it took years to recover the self-esteem I lost that day. It all began one morning when my mother announced she was taking me to visit my father.

"You look so much like Daddy. He misses you, and if he sees you, he might come home."

"Are Linda and Johnny coming?"

"No, just the two of us."

The two of us? It was never just the two of us. Linda would be mad, and Johnny wouldn't understand. I didn't understand either. Where was she taking me?

We had a lot to do to get ready. I polished my black patent shoes until I could see my face in them. I took a bath, and my mother washed my hair.

"I want to curl your hair, so we'll have to dry it," she said.

"No! Please don't make me!" I screamed.

"Stop it. You're acting like a baby."

I hated having my hair dried because we didn't own a hair dryer. Instead, my mother held me over the furnace in the living room floor. When the coils turned red, the heater crackled and popped.

"Please don't drop me," I begged.

I knew she would drop me one day. She wouldn't do it on purpose, but my skin would still crackle and pop like the furnace.

After my hair dried, I put on the brown and white dress Daddy liked – the one he thought matched the color of my hair.

"How long will it take to get there?" I asked as we got in the car.

"Not long. Try to sit still so you'll look nice for Daddy."

We seemed to drive forever, and I was glad when we stopped. I got on my knees and looked out the window. I didn't recognize the building in front of me, but Daddy was standing by the door.

"Daddy!" I yelled.

Mommy opened the car door, and I ran to Daddy. He picked me up, kissed my face and tossed me in the air. I remember how we both laughed and how happy I was he was coming home. After we played, he carried me to a grassy patch and told me to wait there while he and Mommy talked.

I saw some tiny yellow flowers in the grass and picked some for a bouquet. I heard arguing, and when I looked at my parents, Daddy was shaking his head and Mommy was crying. I didn't want her to cry. I wanted to go home.

Daddy began walking toward the building. He was almost to the door when he turned and looked at me. I think he had forgotten I was there. He picked me up and smiled, but he didn't toss me in the air again.

"Daddy loves you," he said.

He kissed my cheek, turned, and walked out of my life.

It was quiet in the car as we drove home. I knew why Mommy wouldn't speak or look at me. It was because I failed her. She thought I could fix what was broken – that I could bring Daddy home – but I couldn't. I wasn't good enough.

Secrecy surrounded my father's disappearance like a dark shroud, and it would be years before I learned the truth behind my parents' divorce. Meanwhile, I struggled with insecurity and guilt - the unintended consequences of my parents' failed marriage.

In 1957, divorce was rare and often scandalous, especially in old, well-established families who lived in small Southern towns. Gossip travels quickly in small places and leaves behind a trail of victims. My mother was one of its wounded, but also a survivor. She accepted responsibility for her children and declined help from her father. Following her divorce, she secured a secretarial position in an office downtown and arranged for Johnny and me to stay with one of our neighbors, Granny McWhorter.

Granny was a kind and gentle soul, but she was old and hard of hearing. My efforts to communicate with her always elicited the same response. She would smile, pat my head and tell me to go play. Her answer implied there was something to play with, but there wasn't. That is, nothing except the burlap sack of alphabet blocks she kept on the floor of her hall closet. Within a week, I exhausted their possibilities and retired them to their home.

Granny spent most of the day in her rocking chair watching a small portable television. Sometimes during *The Price is Right*, she would take her long white hair out of the bun on top of her head and allow me to brush it. At other times, she held her false teeth in the palm of her hand and let me examine them. No one but Granny ever did something like that.

My only playmate was Johnny, but he was content to spend all day making up battles for his plastic soldiers. I admired his ability to create war for so many years with only a handful of those fighting men. Linda was lucky. She was older and went to school. She avoided years of televised morning exercises with Jack LaLanne and afternoons held hostage to soap operas like *The Guiding Light*, *General Hospital* and *The Edge of Night*.

For lack of anything else to do, I spent hours each day sitting in the glider on Granny's front porch rocking back and forth, back and forth. I waited for my mother to rescue me from boredom and for something to change. At last, something did.

My mother received a call from a cousin in Kentucky who invited us to spend the summer on her farm. My mother thought the wide-open space and fresh air might be good for us. In view of the fact her cousin lived on a hog farm, it's dubious her air was any fresher than our own. Still, a visit would give my mother a much-needed respite from her role as a single parent, so off we went.

I was anxious about spending the summer with people I didn't know, but the moment I met Aunt Ellen and Uncle Henry, my worries faded. I could swear they held some secret to happiness that eluded the rest of us. Either that or life on a hog farm just naturally lends itself to a pleasant disposition.

The first thing Uncle Henry taught me was never to climb on a fence that holds hogs. He never said what would happen if I fell in, but from the tone of his voice, it had to be something dreadful. Each day, as I peered through cracks in the fences holding those mammoth beasts, his face would grow serious, and he would warn me,

"Stay away from them hogs. They're mean, and they'll go after ya!"

I could swear those pigs grew more menacing by the day.

Summer ended and before I was ready to go, it was time to leave. A few days before we left, my twelve year old cousin, Ben, offered to buy me ice cream. It sounded like a good idea until I learned it involved walking four miles into town.

As the sweltering midday sun beat down, I put on a brave face and did my best to keep up. On and on we trudged, past row after row of corn. Our footsteps stirred up clouds of dust that stung my eyes and made me cough. I told Ben I was going back to the farm.

"Are you sure you know the way?"

"I'm sure."

With that said, he disappeared down the road without looking back. I stood for a moment and caught my breath, then turned for home. I soon realized I had made a big mistake. One field of corn looks no different from another, and as I passed field after field, I wondered if that hot, dusty road would ever lead me home. Did anyone notice I was missing? Was anyone searching for me? Did anyone care?

I spent the rest of the afternoon trying to find my way back to the farm. I was terrified of being lost in the dark. I came to a fork in the road and stared in both directions. I couldn't waste time, so I chose the road on my left and lumbered ahead.

A familiar sight soon came into view. It was a mailbox I had visited dozens of times that summer. I tried to run, but my legs were sore. When I got closer to the house, I saw everyone standing next to Uncle Henry's truck. He was the first to see me.

"Where have you been, girl? We were about to go searching for you."

"I got lost and couldn't find my way home."

The expression on Uncle Henry's face changed. He ran down the driveway, gathered me in his arms, and stroked my hair.

As we walked towards the house, he whispered, "Don't fret about being lost. You found your way home, and that's what matters."

Ben was sitting on the back porch in a shirt stained with what looked like chocolate ice cream. For someone who'd just had dessert, he didn't look very happy. He kept his eyes fixed on Uncle Henry's face and, as we passed him, Uncle Henry muttered, "I'll get to you later, Ben. You got some explaining to do."

That night, I lay in bed thinking about what Uncle Henry whispered in my ear. Years would pass before I thought of it again, but when I did, I would finally understand what he was trying to say.

Uncle Henry was a good man, kind and generous. Each day as we worked together, laughed and played, I witnessed what a family *could* be and held a picture of it in my mind forever.

The peace I knew at the farm was absent from my home. My maternal grandfather built the house in which I grew up as a wedding gift to my parents. It was on a quaint street in a middle-class neighborhood. We rode our bikes on the sidewalks and played outside until dark. It was a good place to live, but not always a pleasant place to be.

Linda was close to our father, and his disappearance shattered her world. Eventually, her repressed anger turned into unmitigated rage toward our mother. Today, it's common practice for divorcing parents to seek professional help for their children, but it was unheard of in 1957. In those days, divorce was a private matter, rarely discussed even within families.

Linda's outbursts could last for hours and would make sleep impossible. My mother's pleas were futile against the intensity of her tantrums. While these disturbing scenes took place, my little brother lay in his bed crying. Johnny had a gentle nature that made witnessing those confrontations unbearable. I sat on his bed during those nights and tried to calm him.

"Everything will be all right, Johnny. Just close your eyes and go to sleep."

The later it got, the more intolerable the quarreling became. When my mother exhausted every line of reasoning, I intervened, sometimes to the point of physical force, to thwart my sister's hysteria. Eventually, exhaustion would win out, and she would fall asleep sobbing and asking for forgiveness. Linda's anger was a cry for help; she was responding to her overwhelming sense of loss.

One evening, following a particularly disturbing episode, my mother came to my room to tell me goodnight.

"I don't know what I would do without you," she said as she stroked my hair.

I was only seven but already my sister's adversary and my brother's solace. That night I looked at my mother's tired, anxious face and surrendered what was left of my childhood to become her champion. We were the children of an aborted marriage, an abandoned attempt to be a family. In time, we reinvented what family meant, but until then, we each struggled with our feelings in our own way: Linda with explosive anger, Johnny with observable sadness and me with a feigned toughness that hardened my heart.

There were other hurdles to contend with besides our emotional needs, and some of them were equally as daunting. When I was young, I failed to grasp the elusive signs of our less-than-stable financial situation. I was surprised to learn no one else received a free half-gallon of ice cream from the corner market at the end of the month. In reality, the Purity Dairy Neapolitan ice cream we enjoyed was an incentive for my mother to pay her bill in full.

As dire as our situation might have been, I knew we had at least *some* money because I collected it. Following the sudden death of her father three years after her divorce, my mother inherited two houses, eight apartments and a restaurant. For some reason, collecting the rent from each of those places fell on my shoulders. I don't know why my mother entrusted so much responsibility to an 8-year-old child, but it was almost certainly due to necessity rather than forethought.

Each month, before I left to collect the rent, I received a briefing from my mother.

"Miss Ruby's out of work again, so if she can't pay you, tell her it's all right."

Miss Ruby had lived in her apartment since my mother was a girl. She was our favorite tenant, and I knew that even if she never paid us again, she would still have a home. She worked for people who needed help taking care of a loved one in the hospital. If she was out of work, someone was dead.

My mother said it was a gift to serve others, and the Lord had a special place in Heaven just waiting for Miss Ruby. Since she would have to die to reach her special place, I doubted she was in a hurry to claim it.

"Tell the new couple on Woodland Avenue that the plumber is supposed to get by there tomorrow, but one of them will have to be home to let him in."

She kissed the top of my head, grabbed her purse and headed for the door.

"I've got to run or I'll be late. Don't let Mr. Jeffrey frighten you. He likes to tease, but if it bothers you, I'll speak to him."

Mr. Jeffrey ran a restaurant in the building my mother owned on Washington Street. He was a large, ugly man with a loud voice, and I hated him. My mother said it was wrong to hate anyone and if I looked hard enough, I would find good in Mr. Jeffrey. I looked, but it wasn't there.

I picked up the leather satchel with the words *First Trust Bank* printed across the front and tried to tuck it under my arm so nothing would show. I hated walking down the street with that bag. I felt as conspicuous as if *the landlord cometh* was across *my* front.

I arrived at each rental and hoped no one was home. I was shy, and talking to people with whom I had nothing in common was tortuous. I tried to handle any awkward silences by asking the tenants questions about their knickknacks.

Scattered throughout the apartments were collections of teacups, silver spoons, coins, pincushions, dolls, ashtrays and more. Every month, I listened to the same stories about the history of each treasure.

I dreaded two places more than all the others. One was Mr. Jeffrey's restaurant, and the other was an apartment in the rear of the same building.

I always went to the restaurant first so I could put the experience behind me as soon as possible.

My trips to collect Mr. Jeffrey's rent weren't haphazard visits. I had my technique down to a science, but in spite of my best efforts, the same thing always happened. I would open the door of the restaurant without making a sound and move across the crowded dining room so quietly that no one was even aware of my presence. Mr. Jeffrey would always be standing at the bar on the opposite side of the room, and the second he saw me he would bellow, "Here she is again, folks. My little landlord wants her rent. What do you suppose she does with all that money?"

Everyone in the restaurant would look at me and laugh. I would grab Mr. Jeffrey's rent and race out the door. It was devastating to be the butt of his joke.

Next, I would go around to the back of the building and climb twenty rickety steps to the apartment on the second floor. By the time I reached the top, my heart was pounding like a hammer. When I knocked on the door, a gnarled old woman would open it and motion for me to enter. Like a scene straight from an Alfred Hitchcock movie, I took a deep breath and crossed the threshold into her surreal world.

The walls of her apartment held dozens of shelves displaying her strange obsession: crocheted dishes. White plates decorated in green, pink cups trimmed in white, bowls and platters; everywhere I turned, I saw crocheted dishes starched as stiff as cardboard so they would resemble the real thing. The old woman had to be crazy to sit all day creating bogus tableware. Every time I entered her apartment, I feared I would be murdered, starched and put on display.

Every month the old woman placed a crochet hook in my hand and instructed me on how to create a cup and saucer. It was terrifying to sit there as she pulled on the threads and inspected my handiwork.

"No, no," she'd cry in her shrill, nervous voice, "that's not how it's done!"

Luckily, it never took long for her to tire of my inability to follow directions, and the moment she did, I hastily made an excuse to leave. As we walked to the door, she always reached in the pocket of her dress and retrieved a small lavender envelope with the word *rent* scribbled across the front. I took it from her bony hand, placed it in the satchel and ran all the way home. I never relaxed until I deposited our fresh supply of money on top of my mother's dresser.

The tenants changed over the years, but I still made the same trip each month to collect the rent. I never learned what happened to the money, but my mother wasn't one to exaggerate. If she said there was no money to spare, then there wasn't.

THE BOTTOM OF THE BARREL 3

What's it all about? Every day, Dionne Warwick's soulful recording of *Alfie* blasted through the closed door of my bedroom as I searched my soul for the answer. I convinced myself all the disappointments of my childhood would be rectified once I became a teenager. I imagined turning into someone special, but instead, I grew callous, cynical and indifferent. I abandoned faith and gave up hope, two formidable forces I could well have used in my corner.

If there are advantages to growing up in a small town, I never discovered them. I blamed my restlessness on the fact that I lived in a place where the highlight of the summer was the Saturday night dances held at the local skating rink. When my mother learned young soldiers from a nearby military base were attending, she denied me even that small pleasure. I considered my new restriction overly harsh and used that reasoning to justify disobeying her. I only made that mistake once.

It seemed to me that Linda's first priority in life was making sure I was miserable. When she learned I had broken my mother's rule and gone to a dance, she informed on me and even volunteered to drive my mother to the skating rink. The sight of them standing in front of all my friends and ordering me to the car remains seared in my mind forever. When I confronted Linda about her betrayal, she smiled and said it was for my own good. The next day when her boyfriend called, I told him she had left town. It was for her own good.

Raising three teenagers would be challenging under any circumstances, but as a single parent, my mother found it an especially daunting responsibility. I try not to judge her actions, but a few of them defy logic and therefore qualify as fair game.

As a teenager, Linda's blond hair and blue eyes caught the attention of every boy in town. My mother wrestled with how best to safeguard her from improper advances and, in what I have come to believe was a temporary mental breakdown due to stress, reasoned that my presence on Linda's dates would deter those advances. As a result, Linda was not allowed to go out at night unless I accompanied her. Naturally, she resented my constant presence, and it exacerbated our already fragile relationship. On the other hand, I enjoyed becoming a part of her circle of friends. They had access to what all teenagers dream of – cars.

If my mother had recognized my vulnerability, she would never have placed me in such a precarious position. She failed to anticipate that boys, both Linda's age and older, would be interested in someone as young as fourteen, but they were, and her oversight had disastrous consequences.

At first, the attention I received from these older, more mature boys bolstered my self-confidence. I was wanted, needed and loved – all the things for which I longed. I thought their feelings were as genuine as my own, but they weren't. They read my heart like a book and knew exactly what part to play.

My immaturity and need for approval led me from one reckless relationship to another. None of them was genuine, most were harmful and all of them ended abruptly. When they did, a voice inside my head reminded me that it was my fault. I wasn't good enough. If I were, they wouldn't have left. After a while, I stopped feeling anything for anyone. Eventually, nothing hurt.

I was drowning in the bottom of a barrel but didn't know how far I had sunk until the day I met Danny Cockerel. We met at a party when I was fifteen and he was a sophomore in college. It was one of those gatherings that just happen – most often, when someone's parents are out of town. However, this party was different. It wasn't in the basement room of a friend's home; it was in a house rented by some boys who attended the local college. It was a place notorious for harboring drugs, and Danny was a boy known for selling them.

I didn't want to be there. I asked a friend to drop me off elsewhere, but she begged me not to abandon her and I yielded. It was a poor decision. The night was anything but fun. I was accustomed to impetuous behavior but not the level of depravity around me. There appeared to no restraint to the sex, drugs and alcohol offered. I opted out of everything except a Vodka Collins I nursed all evening.

The *friend* I came with – the one who begged me not to abandon her – disappeared within minutes, and I didn't search for fear of what I might find. I was standing in the kitchen when I saw a couple of friends come through the back door. It was a relief to join them.

"What are you doing here?" my friend Mike asked.

Before I could answer, I heard a voice behind me.

"Hey, sweet thing, I've been trying to talk to you all night."

I turned and looked into the dazed eyes of a boy so drunk he could barely stand. I knew who he was. Everyone knew who Danny Cockerel was. Reputations as bad as his are the basis for folklore in small towns. Still – something about his bleached blonde hair and dark complexion created a certain level of attractiveness.

"Are you speaking to me?"

"Hell yeah, I've been trying to catch up with you all night, but I keep losing you."

Considering we were in Danny's own small off-campus house, his inability to navigate familiar ground was probably due to his drinking. In the course of the evening, he had consumed a half-liter of Vodka, numerous shots of whiskey, two bourbon and cokes and most of the gin and tonic in his hand – not that I cared or was paying attention.

"Is there something you want?"

"Yeah, you could say that."

He moved closer and I could smell the whiskey on his breath. In spite of his smile, something in his eyes frightened me, and I took a step closer to Mike.

"Leave her alone, Danny," Mike said.

"Who are you, her Daddy?"

I stepped between them in an effort to diffuse the ugly situation rapidly developing. Mike was several years older than I was, and protective in the way a big brother is of a sister. I had heard stories about the way Danny dealt with his grudges, and I didn't want Mike added to his hate list.

"Danny, I wish we could stay, but it's late, and if I'm not home in the next 30 minutes, my crazy mother will have the entire family out looking for me. Thanks for the party. It's been great."

I grabbed Mike's arm and pulled him towards the door. He clenched his fists and never took his eyes off Danny. When we got outside, I hugged him around his waist and felt his heart pounding.

"You didn't need to do that. I can take care of myself, but not both of us."

"I wouldn't say that. I think you did a damn good job."

I looked at him and we both burst into laughter. By the time we stopped, we were sitting on the pavement leaning against someone's car and wiping our eyes.

"Would you actually have fought for me?"

"I guess neither of us will ever know."

We looked at each other and laughed again. When we stopped, Mike put his arm around my shoulder, and I laid my head against his chest.

"Stay away from Cockerel. He's bad news, and you shouldn't be hanging around him or this house. You may think you can take care of yourself, but you're wrong. Cockerel gets what he wants."

"First of all, it wasn't my idea to come here. Secondly, I hope I never see Danny Cockerel again. There's something dark about him that scares me."

"I think he's too drunk to remember anything about tonight, but just the same, stay away from here."

Mike jumped to his feet and held out his hands.

"Come on. I've got to get you home before your crazy mother has the entire family out looking for you.'"

We laughed as Mike pulled me to my feet. His back was to the house, so he didn't see what I saw. Danny was standing on the other side of the screen door glaring at us. I had no idea how long he had been there, or what he had seen or heard, but the look on his face was harrowing. I should have told Mike, but I had already put him through a lot. Besides, he was probably right. Danny was too drunk to remember anything.

I took Mike's hand and we walked down the street towards his car. We hadn't gone far when I glanced over my shoulder at the house again. Danny was still standing there, and I knew he would remember every detail of that night.

Two things happened the following week that rattled both Mike and me. On Tuesday, someone smashed the windshield of Mike's car. The car was sitting in the parking lot at school, but no one saw or heard anything suspicious. That same night, I started receiving disturbing calls from boys I had never met. They used coarse language and made ugly insinuations. I hung up on each of them; even so, I was too upset to sleep and cried most of the night.

The calls continued all week and grew more and more offensive. It was obvious to my mother something was going on. How could she not notice my new popularity among boys? Fortunately, she didn't ask questions because I had no answers.

Mike called on Friday and told me someone slashed a tire on his car while he was at work. We agreed to meet the next morning to talk about what was happening.

"Tell me the truth. Do you think this has something to do with last weekend?"

Mike took a sip of his soft drink before he answered.

"This has Cockerel written all over it. The calls are his way of freaking you out. If I had to guess, he probably wrote your name and number on a wall."

"What wall?"

"It's just a thing guys do."

"What are you talking about?"

"In a lot of houses, especially frat houses, guys leave info on the wall next to the phone about girls other guys might like."

"What do you mean 'girls other guys might like'?"

The second the words left my mouth, I understood what he was trying to say.

"Do you mean whores? Danny Cockerel put my name and number on a whore wall?"

"It's not called a 'whore wall.' Anyway, you don't have to worry about getting more calls. I'm going over to campus this afternoon, and when I find where he wrote it, I'll get rid of it. It won't be hard. There's only a few places it could be."

"What about your car?"

"Smashed windshields and slashed tires are Cockerel's calling cards. Someone I know who was at the party said Cockerel was so mad after we left he threw a can of beer through a window. I guess I was wrong about him not remembering."

"It's my fault. If it weren't for me, none of this would be happening to you."

"Whoa! This isn't your fault. You may have been in the wrong place at the wrong time, but this guy's crazy. No one goes around doing stuff like this unless he's nuts."

"Or evil. I told you there's something dark about him."

"Don't be scared. A friend of mine delivered a message to Cockerel for me last night. I told him if he caused either of us any more trouble, we'd file charges against him. He may be crazy, but he won't risk getting kicked out of school – not with Vietnam looming in front of him. Besides, my friend can be pretty persuasive."

"Who is he?"

"Randy Shriver. *Deputy* Randy Shriver. He graduated from the police academy last year."

I looked at Mike, and we both burst into laughter.

The obscene phone calls ended, Mike replaced the windshield and tire on his car, and even though I continued to make poor decisions, none of them ever took me to a place like Danny Cockerel's house again. I learned not to look for happiness in dark places. Besides, just because the barrel had sprung a leak this time didn't mean it would happen again. It was best not to push my luck.

SECOND CHANCES 4

Following the disturbing episode with Danny, my unfocused rebellion waned, but not my recklessness. I tried my mother's patience at every turn, pushed the limits and devised creative excuses to cover my tracks. A typical conversation between us went something like this:

"I found your belt laying outside your window this morning," said my mother.

Her back was to me as she stirred a pot of oatmeal on the stove.

"Oh, I almost forgot. I woke up last night soaked in sweat and tried to force open the window next to my bed. I had almost given up when suddenly it shot up and knocked me off balance. I fell against the screen, and it came loose and landed outside. I tried to snag it with my belt so I could haul it back in, but I dropped the belt. Please buy me a fan. I don't know how you expect me to get any sleep. The heat in that room is unbearable."

My mother reached across the breakfast table, handed me my belt and began buttering the toast. I almost felt sorry for her. How could anyone believe a crazy story like that? I was silently applauding my ingenuity and quick response when she asked another question.

"How did the screen get back in your window? It was there this morning."

"I climbed out the window to find my belt, but it was too dark, so I picked up the screen and pushed it through the window. When I got back inside, I hung it up."

"Did all of this happen before or after you came home at two o'clock this morning?"

My mother was good at throwing a curve when I least expected it. In a brazen act of disrespect, I took another spoonful of oatmeal before I spoke.

"I don't know what you mean."

"Oh, I think you do. I just got off the phone with one of our neighbors. Around two o'clock this morning, her dog started barking. She checked outside and was surprised to find a car parked in front of her house. She was even more surprised when she saw *you* get out. Maybe *I* should get a dog – a watchdog."

I admired my mother's stubborn resolve to confront my insolence. She had a way of getting her message across without threats or reprimands. She didn't need to say it. I knew my days of sneaking out the window were over.

Although my mother thought she knew the truth about that night, she didn't. If she had, she wouldn't have dismissed the matter so quickly. On the night in question, I climbed out my bedroom window and met friends two blocks away. We spent the next several hours in a fruitless quest for adventure. It took years for us to understand we would never find adventure in that small town because none would ever exist – not unless we created it.

"I'll ride with Mike," I shouted.

I squeezed into the back seat of Mike's 1968 Camaro, and we headed to the construction site for a new bridge across the river. For the time being, it ended midway across the Cumberland, and the only thing preventing cars from driving onto it was a sawhorse barricade. A friend noticed this flimsy roadblock one night and invented the game in which we were about to take part.

Cars began to arrive and lined up one behind the other. The fun started when the driver in front of the line floored the gas pedal in his car and took off toward the bridge. Once he used his brakes, he couldn't use the gas again. The winner of the game was the driver whose car stopped closest to the end of the bridge in the shortest amount of time.

Mike's car was in front that night, and as he clutched the steering wheel and floored the gas all eyes stared at the road ahead. We were reckless but not fearless. As the bridge came in sight, someone yelled it was straight ahead.

"I see it!" Mike shouted.

Why wasn't he using the brake? It would be too late if he waited until we reached the bridge.

"Mike, stop the car!" I screamed.

No one noticed the bridge was still wet from the rain earlier in the evening. When Mike slammed on the brake, his car went into a violent tailspin that sent us crashing into the side of the bridge. I screamed as my body was hurled from one side of the car to the other. When we finally stopped, there was nothing but silence. Mike sounded frantic as he tried to determine if anyone was hurt.

"Is everyone all right? I tried to stop the car. I didn't know the bridge was wet."

One by one, we piled out of the car. My legs shook, but as I examined the scene in front of me, they trembled even harder. Mike's car was sideways, and had stopped only a foot from the end of the bridge.

I stood in the dark looking at the car and listening to the murmur of voices around me. Someone said we were lucky to be alive. Others questioned why we had all risked so much. I didn't have questions. I knew why I was there. From the time I woke up until the minute I went to bed,

I searched for something to replace the boredom and emptiness I felt. I wanted to believe there was more to life, but if there was, I couldn't see it.

Someone offered me a ride home, and I accepted. It was around two o'clock in the morning when a friend dropped me off a few blocks from home. After countless attempts to climb back through my bedroom window, I finally peeled off my tight jeans, wiggled through and collapsed on the bed. Unfortunately, fatigue left me careless, and I forgot to retrieve my belt - the same belt my unflappable mother had just presented to me at the breakfast table.

There was a time when school helped fill the emptiness, but not anymore. It hindered my social life. I skipped classes and learned to manipulate my curfew by spending the night with friends. I thought I was clever until I developed a severe case of infectious mononucleosis, (a.k.a. the kissing disease.) It was a common illness at my high school though not this severe.

I knew something was wrong, but I refused to complain for fear it might jeopardize my newest relationship. Within a week, my condition worsened, and I could barely walk. At home, I crawled to the bathroom (as the middle child, I was almost invisible).

When it was time to leave for school, I took a deep breath, gathered all my strength and walked out the door. The second I boarded the bus, I lay my head against the window and slept. My charade finally ended when I woke one morning unable to stand or speak. When my mother came to check on me, her face turned pale.

"What's wrong? You look terrible."

"I can't get up," I whispered.

My temperature registered 103, and we were in the car and on our way to the hospital before I could grab my robe. A blood sample confirmed I had mononucleosis, and another test indicated an enlarged spleen. My doctor sentenced me to six weeks of bed rest and threatened hospitalization if I didn't cooperate.

If not for the homebound teacher who came each week to help me with my assignments, I would have failed the semester. As it was, I lost the boyfriend I worked so hard to keep. Within days of my absence, he disappeared. My experience should have taught me a lesson, but it didn't. I returned to school as defiant as ever.

I was sitting in Marsolete Welker's English class one morning when she received a note instructing me to report to the principal's office. As usual, I took my time getting there.

I arrived at Principal Howard Thompson's (a.k.a. Big Tom) office and found my friend, Cheri, sitting in the chair next to him. He motioned for me to sit down, and then pushed a note across his desk until it lay in front of me.

"Did you write this?" he asked.

It was a letter from Cheri's mother stating Cheri had been absent from school due to an illness. I was on the verge of denying I had ever seen it when I remembered an incident that occurred weeks earlier. I was standing at my locker one morning when Cheri approached me for help. She had typed a note and wanted me to sign her mother's signature to it.

"Why don't you sign it yourself?"

"They're not stupid. It wouldn't take them long to figure out it's my handwriting. I need someone else to sign it."

It seemed harmless, so I complied. I glanced at Cheri, but she diverted her eyes.

"Forging someone's signature is a serious offense," Big Tom said.

Why was Cheri so quiet? Why didn't she say something? Then it hit me. I wouldn't be in Big Tom's office unless she had already told him I signed the note.

"Cheri asked me to sign it so she wouldn't get in trouble for skipping school."

"Apparently, she doesn't care if *you* get in trouble."

Big Tom told Cheri to wait outside his office. He came around his desk, closed the door and sat down beside me. I had known Big Tom for as long as I could remember. When I was younger, he was our neighbor. Out of respect for my mother, he had let me off the hook on more than one occasion.

"I'm not sure why you associate with some of the people you do, but your mother deserves better from you. You're walking down a dead-end road, and it's time you changed direction."

"Are you going to suspend me?"

"No, I'm not letting you off that easy. I'm calling your mother."

I left Big Tom's office and looked for Rick. I found him sitting alone in the cafeteria. I worried about our relationship. Although we had only dated a few months, I knew he had serious feelings for me – feelings I didn't reciprocate.

I'm not sure what he saw in me. We were complete opposites. He was thoughtful; I was self-centered. He was cautious; I was daring. He was responsible; I was reckless. He was a serious student, and I couldn't have cared less. I was everything he should have disliked but for some reason didn't. On the contrary, from our first date onward, I had his unwavering devotion.

I wanted to be honest about my feelings, but I convinced myself that in time he would see for himself we didn't belong together. How could we? I was a taker, and he was a giver. He gave me more of himself than I deserved, and I knew that eventually he would end up hurt. I cut across the cafeteria and told him about my encounter with Big Tom.

"What I can't understand is why Cheri told him I signed the note. She could have said *she* did it, or refused to say who did. Why did she have to get me in trouble?"

Rick listened to everything I said, and then, in an uncharacteristic outburst, threw down his fork and looked straight into my eyes.

"She did it because she doesn't care about you. The only person she cares about is herself. Most of your friends are the same way."

His words felt like a slap across my face, but he was right. Most of my friends were self-centered and callous – just like me.

"Maybe it's because they've been hurt by people like you who say they care when they really don't."

I felt tears run down my face, and he handed me his handkerchief.

"I care and you know it."

"Well, you should find someone else to care about – someone who needs you because *I* don't. I don't need anyone. I'm no different from my friends. I use people to get what I want, and they use me to get what they want. That's the way things work."

"No, that's the way you *think* things work. You expect the worst from everyone, including yourself, but it doesn't have to be that way."

"Maybe not for you, but that's how it is for me. You think you know me, but you don't. You don't know anything about the mistakes I've made."

"Everyone makes mistakes. Some people make more than others do, but you're *not* like your friends. If you were, I would have left a long time ago."

I stopped crying and listened to words I had waited all my life to hear.

"I've loved you since the day we met, but all you do is push me away. I think you're afraid of love. I don't know why that is, but you can trust me. I won't let you down, and I won't leave."

I was speechless. It was as if he could read my heart and see straight into my soul. He wasn't the person I had dreamed of hearing those words from, and yet over time he had become my best friend. Being with him gave me a sense of peace I had never experienced with anyone else. I knew it wasn't love, but I thought someday it might be. It was worth a chance... *he* was worth a chance.

I avoided my old friends and wasn't surprised to discover they didn't care. I stopped skipping school and started studying. As my GPA rose, so did my confidence and I soon found myself emulating the same qualities in Rick I once loathed. He reminded me of something I had almost forgotten. Something whispered in my ear a long time ago, "Don't fret over being lost. You found your way home, and that's what matters."

Life stopped hurting, and I began thinking about the future.

THE OPPORTUNITY OF A LIFETIME 5

Senior year arrived and anxiety set in. The question on everyone's mind was *what next*. Most of my friends were looking for jobs or looking to get married. I wasn't motivated in either direction, so I set my sights on college. It sounded like a lot more fun than having a full-time job or being someone's wife.

My mother pulled together over a dozen scholarship applications, all of which required me to invent unique reasons why I, versus someone else, deserved the money needed to attend college. Words like *conscientious* and *indomitable* flowed unapologetically from my pen.

"Without a scholarship, is there any way for me to go to college?" I asked.

"Let's not worry about that. Just focus on these forms. Things always work out somehow." That was my mother – practical, yet full of faith.

The following week, I stumbled upon a different type of application – one that had nothing to do with college but everything to do with adventure. I discovered it one Sunday posted on the bulletin board next to the front door of our church:

Forty students will attend this year's United Nations Study Tour. Only residents of Tennessee may apply. Academic performance, recommendations and a personal essay are the criteria for selection. The essay is limited to 1000 words and must address what you hope to achieve by participating in the Study Tour.

At seventeen, the only thing I hoped to achieve was escaping from the small town I called home. The application I stared at represented the unexpected opportunity of a lifetime. Printed across the top of the page were the words: *The United Nations Study Tour,* but it was the second line that stopped me in my tracks: *New York City.* Although my prior travel experiences provided no temptation to leave the green hills I called home, New York did. It was the place where everything happened . . . at least according to *16 Magazine.* I removed the application from the bulletin board and stuck it in my purse. I was determined not to let this opportunity slip away.

Between applying for college scholarships, I worked on getting to New York. Several prominent citizens in town agreed to serve as references, and their letters had recently arrived. As I read each one, I wondered if the authors had confused me with someone else. Every letter referred to my exemplary character and gave wholehearted support for my effort to expand my horizons. Regardless of the reasons behind their generous words, I was grateful for their support.

I knew if I hoped to achieve a spot on the Study Tour, my essay would have to stand out from among all the others. I worked tirelessly, but all my attempts to create something inspirational, earnest or captivating ended up the same way – in the garbage. Everything I wrote sounded desperate and contrived.

With less than a week before the application deadline, I was still struggling. Explaining why I was applying and what I hoped to achieve was difficult. I wanted to experience a place where life could be reinvented every day. New York was the opposite of *here,* and that alone made it reason to forge ahead.

It was after midnight when I ripped another fruitless stab at creativity from my notebook and tossed it in the trash. The application deadline was within days, but I had yet to create anything close to satisfactory, much less exceptional.

I went to bed depressed. It was gut wrenching to surrender hope of going on the Study Tour. My eyes filled with tears, and I reached for a tissue. In the process, I knocked over the picture on my bedside table. It was a photograph of my mother, and although it had sat next to my bed for as long as I could remember, I had never noticed how young she looked. As I studied her face, words that had eluded me for weeks began to take shape.

I got out of bed, turned on the light and started writing. My numerous college scholarship essays had helped me perfect a vivid description of my potential greatness, but that night I set aside my artful knack for obscuring the truth and concentrated on being honest. The composition I wrote was about my mother and the sacrifices she made in order to give me a chance at my dreams. I wanted her to know those sacrifices were worth the price she paid.

The morning light was creeping into my room when I placed the essay inside a large envelope to mail later that day. I climbed in bed and looked once again at the picture of my mother. In spite of her own sacrifices, she didn't ask much from me. Attending church was her only mandatory and non-negotiable rule. The past week's sermon was based on the verse: *Good things come to those who wait.* My mother had waited a long time to see something good come from her investment in me, and as I looked at the envelope on my desk, I hoped she wouldn't have to wait much longer.

Each day, I watched for the mail and hoped for a reply to my application. Weeks passed without any response, and I grew less and less optimistic. At the end of the fifth week, I stopped checking the mail. I had given it my best shot but it wasn't enough. I decided to put the entire experience behind me.

Days later, I was lying on my bed listening to Dionne sing when Linda poked her head in my room.

"There's a letter for you in the mail. I put it on the desk."

I ran to the living room and snatched up the mail. On the bottom of the pile, I found a letter addressed to me. I glanced at the return address and saw it was from the church.

I had alternately hoped and dreaded for this day to arrive. I prepared for the worst, and then opened the envelope.

"Congratulations on being selected to attend this year's United Nations Study Tour."

I couldn't believe what I read. Was it a mistake? Should I call and ask for confirmation? I examined the envelope again and saw my name and address printed across the front. It was true. I was going to New York! I believe in luck, but this went beyond luck. As I stood looking at the letter in my hand, I knew it was a miracle.

That evening, when my mother arrived home, I met her at the door and threw my arms around her.

"What's this about?" she asked.

"Mom, sit down. You won't believe what's happened. It's a miracle."

The price tag on my unexpected opportunity of a lifetime was two hundred dollars. How I managed to overlook this critical detail is a mystery to me since much of my life revolved around money, or, to be more precise, the lack of it. During my teenage years, our budget was so constricted even clothes were off-limits.

"We can't afford to shop for clothes, but if you learn to sew, I'll supply all the patterns and fabric you need," my mother said.

I tried but never mastered the art of sewing. I had plenty of determination but not enough patience. I never figured out the proper way to attach a sleeve to a dress, and my attempts always yielded the same result – mass amounts of material gathered in bulky folds in the armpits of everything I made. It was mortifying to think I might forget one day and raise my hand in class.

Under circumstances such as these, it's hard to imagine how something as significant as the cost of the Study Tour escaped my attention. Maybe I just wanted to avoid thinking about it or, on the other hand, reasoned that if I weren't selected, there would be no *need* to think about it. Regardless, I should have given the cost more consideration. The deadline for submitting the fee was imminent, and I had to come up with the money.

When I approached my mother for help, her immediate response was, "Ask your father." That was her standard reply to all requests outside our budget. I had legitimate reasons to dislike asking my father for money. To begin with, I hardly knew him. Since my parents' divorce thirteen years before, my only connection with my father was through his occasional calls and letters. Additionally, any requests for funds suggested a *you owe it to me* sentiment that I found repugnant. Given my memory of the last time I saw my father, it's little wonder I avoided contacting him. My mother, however, was adamant.

"You've got to write your father today. You don't have time to put this off any longer," she said before leaving the house.

The registration fee for the Study Tour was due within weeks, and with the standard rate of a babysitter being only fifty cents an hour, I had little chance of earning enough money on my own. Left with no alternative, I wrote to my father. A week later, I received his reply along with a folded twenty-dollar bill. When I showed it to my mother, she looked disappointed but attempted a brave response.

"Don't worry. Things always work out somehow." That was my mother at her best.

Later that week, I found myself studying the faces of the women gathered in our church parlor. They were present for the monthly meeting of the United Methodist Women. These were the true saints of the church. Their lives centered on doing good works and helping those in need. At present, *I* was in need – in need of another hundred dollars to cover the cost of the Study Tour. It wasn't as if I had sat idly by waiting for money to fall into my lap. I had done every job available, but it wasn't enough. If I didn't have the money by next week, I would have to forfeit my spot on the tour.

I was worried about the reaction to my request. Would the women consider it selfish and disrespectful to suggest they reroute money for the poor to help me go on a trip? Would they think I was shameless and greedy? Maybe they would turn me out of the church. What was I thinking? Why should these women want to help a self-centered teenage girl explore New York? I glanced around for the nearest exit but realized the meeting was about to begin.

After reading the minutes from the previous month, the secretary asked about new business. The president, Mrs. Lenora Manning, rose to her feet and announced a guest was present with a special request to make.

I stood and thanked the women for allowing me to speak. I reminded them I was baptized in that church and had attended every event open to the membership since the day I was born. I may have even announced my intention of becoming a future member of the United Methodist Women. (I offer no defense for my shameless attempt to acquire the money). I spoke about the Study Tour and its benefits for a small-town girl, how it would give me a broader perspective of the world and a vision for the future.

When I finished speaking, those saints of the church rose to their feet and applauded. Mrs. Manning, her arm around my shoulder, called for a motion to provide me the money I needed and it passed unanimously. Everyone expressed her sincerest wish for a safe and valuable experience.

I offered my heartfelt thanks, excused myself from the meeting, and raced to the nearest exit.

I needed air . . . maybe I needed to hide. I looked over my shoulder to make sure no one had followed. The women hadn't gone ballistic. They thought the trip was a worthwhile use of their money. That's when it finally hit me. I had the money I needed and I was going to New York City!

I recalled the conversation I had with my mother when she first suggested I ask the women of the church for help.

"There's no reason for them to even consider it," I said.

"Yes, there is. They'll help because they care."

"Why should they care whether I go to New York?"

"It's not about New York. It's about you. They care about you."

Usually, I ignored my mother's advice. After all, I was seventeen. I reached in my purse and took out the keys to our car. I could hardly wait to get home and tell her the news. As I backed out of the parking lot, I wondered if it might be a good idea to ask what she thought I should take to New York.

BEYOND THE LINCOLN TUNNEL 6

New York! Part of me was afraid I would wake up one morning and discover I was dreaming. To remind myself it was real, I cut out the letters *N, E, W, Y, O, R,* and *K* and glued them to the inside of my closet door. As soon as Linda saw them, she informed my mother, but as much to my surprise as hers, she said they could stay. I never loved my mother more than when she stood up on my behalf. However, in this case, the glue didn't leave her much choice.

The next month passed in a flurry of activity. I doubled up on assignments from school, planned my wardrobe and poured over a battered copy of a New York City guidebook I checked out from our local library. New York! I could hardly think of anything else.

The official itinerary for the Study Tour soon arrived, and a new thought crashed into my mind: I would be in New York in less than a week — but without Rick.

That weekend, I spent most of our regular Saturday night date talking about the agenda for the Study Tour. Rick was supportive of the trip, but the more I said, the quieter he became. At last, my comments dwindled into silence.

"Rick, I wish you were going with me. I'll miss you, but this is the opportunity of a lifetime. I can't just pass it up."

He stared straight ahead through the windshield of his car. More silence. More staring. Rick has always been a person who thoughtfully prepares his words before he voices them. Most of the time I just found it annoying, but tonight it was downright agonizing. Finally, he turned and looked at me.

"I don't want you to pass up the trip. That's the last thing I would ever want. I was just thinking about how lonely it will be without you."

His candor surprised me. He rarely shared his feelings – even with me.

"I'll only be away a short time, and I'll write every day. You won't even know I'm gone."

His eyes never left mine.

"I'll know, Nancy," he said.

The look on his face told me everything he couldn't say. My eyes welled with tears, and a lump in my throat made it impossible to speak. He leaned across the center console of the car and kissed me.

"I'll miss you every day you're away," he said.

I spent that night staring at the ceiling. Rick saved my life. His patience, his wisdom and his unwavering faith in me helped me reclaim my self-respect. Without him, I would never have attained the grades or confidence to apply for the Study Tour, much less be accepted. Ironically, what he helped me achieve was now pulling us apart.

Rick had to work the day I left for the Study Tour, so we said goodbye on the phone.

"Try not to replace me while you're away," he said.

"Don't be ridiculous. I'll only be gone a short time, and if the itinerary is correct, I'll be in classes all day. Even if I wanted to meet someone else, there wouldn't be time."

"Is that supposed to be reassuring? Don't forget to write and don't forget I love you."

"I'll remember both."

My mother used our drive to Nashville as an opportunity to give last-minute instructions.

"Remember to take lots of pictures and send everyone a postcard."

"I will."

"Don't forget long distance calls are expensive, so only phone if it's absolutely necessary,"

"I won't."

I was relieved when we reached our destination and my mother's endless advice ceased. The driveway of the church where we had just arrived led us to a large parking area. Sitting in the middle of the parking lot, surrounded by mounds of suitcases, duffel bags and backpacks was a Greyhound Bus. There was no scarcity of hovering parents, and it was amusing to watch the tactics used to hurry them on their way.

I made my way through the sea of unfamiliar faces to a makeshift registration table. A middle-aged man whose nametag identified him as Peter, our chaperone and director of the Study Tour, searched his list for my name. I held my breath and waited for confirmation this wasn't all a big mistake.

"Let's see . . . Yep. Here you are."

I relaxed for the first time since leaving home that morning. I was on the list!

Peter drew a line through my name and tossed me an enormous manila envelope.

"The materials inside are for your classes on Monday. You can use our travel time to familiarize yourself with them."

I looked at the size of the packet and began to have second thoughts about the Study Tour. I planned to use my travel time to catch up on the latest pop magazine, not prepare for school.

My mother pulled me aside just as the last of our bags were shoved into the belly of the Greyhound bus. Despite assuring her I would be fine, her goodbye hug left me feeling as if she doubted we would ever see each other again. As she pulled out of the parking lot and waved goodbye, a yoke of sadness descended on me, and my so-called self-confidence morphed into fear.

With my information packet tucked under one arm, and the patchwork purse I had carried since ninth grade hanging from the other, I climbed the steps of the bus and sank into my assigned seat. Luckily, I didn't have time to spiral down into a full-blown case of the blues. I had barely put my belongings away when the boy in the seat next to me introduced himself.

"Hi! I'm Joey. I guess we're going to be seatmates on this journey of a thousand miles. Pretty exciting, huh? I've never been to New York, but my parents say it's the greatest city in the world. Except for Nashville, of course. I'm from Nashville. Where are you from?"

I stared at him. He had just said more words in one minute than Rick had in two years of dating. His grin slowly collapsed.

"What's the matter? Is it something I said?"

"No. I've just never met anyone who talks as fast as I do."

Joey had broad shoulders, a mop of curly dark hair and blue eyes that sparkled every time he smiled.

"My name is Nancy, and I'm from Clarksville."

"I've never heard of Clarksville, so you'll have to tell me all about it."

"That won't take long."

"Don't worry. I have a feeling we'll find plenty to talk about."

Joey was right. We spent the next fourteen hours in non-stop conversation. He was as good a listener as he was a talker and so open and engaging that no topic seemed off-limits. I had never met anyone quite like him, and yet I felt like we had known each other all our lives. The high school he attended was a well-known private academy for boys. Although he didn't display an ounce of pretentiousness, I suspected the cost of our trip wasn't nearly as challenging for him as it was for me.

It was past midnight when our Greyhound rolled into a budget motel outside of Washington, D.C. Our collective mood was much quieter as we unloaded the bus and collected our luggage. Peter handed each of us the next day's schedule and announced our room assignments. My roommate was Kara. She lived in Memphis but was originally from Atlanta. Her thick Southern drawl made me smile whenever she spoke, and I knew within minutes of meeting her that I had found a friend.

"Do you need help with your bags?" Joey asked as we shuffled off to our room.

I was beat, but it was too much to ask.

"No, I can manage."

"Are you sure? They look heavy, and I don't mind helping."

"I'll be okay, but thanks for asking."

Joey smiled and despite the late hour and unfamiliar surroundings, his eyes still sparkled.

"Well, if you're sure, then I'll see you in the morning."

I couldn't help checking him out as he walked away. His faded Levi's and white Oxford shirt hugged all the right places. Guiltily, I recalled the phone conversation I had with Rick just that morning.

"Try not to replace me while you're away."

What was I thinking?

Kara and I managed to drag our bags up two flights of stairs and into our dark room. It was a close call as to which of us crawled in bed first. I pulled the covers up to my chin trying to compensate for the broken radiator across the room. I was glad it was too late to write. When I did get around to writing, I resolved not to mention Joey. Rick would only worry, and there was no need for that . . . or was there?

I doubt any group of people ever came together so completely in such a short amount of time as the forty of us did the following day. The closer we got to Manhattan, the more animated our conversations became.

"Look! There's the Lincoln Tunnel," someone shouted.

Everyone grew silent as our bus merged with traffic and entered the tunnel. There was a sense of reverence to the experience that created the odd sensation of entering a sacred space.

The tunnel was longer than I expected, and I was glad when we reached the end. Sunlight filled the bus the moment we exited, and my senses exploded. The profusion of people, cars, buildings and noise left me speechless. The city was busting at the seams, but I sensed order in the chaos.

As our Greyhound ventured farther into the city, I looked from one place to another trying to take in every sight. Joey laughed at my enthusiasm, but it was obvious he found the city equally as exciting. We stared out the window together and began making plans to explore the world outside our bus.

New York was even more riveting, outrageous and spectacular than I had imagined. Yet instead of being intimidated, I felt as if I had stepped out of an ill-fitting skin and into one customized just for me.

I thought our classes at the United Nations would be superficial and boring, but I was wrong. The topics we covered were complicated but also relevant and stimulating. I dived into subjects I never imagined discussing: national interests versus global ethics, oil dependency and America's involvement in Southeast Asia. I began rethinking my blasé attitude toward learning and wondered if my long-term indifference to school might be the result of classes I found dull and immaterial.

We had been in New York for several days when Peter announced he had purchased tickets for the Broadway production of *The Me Nobody Knows*. Attending a Broadway show was beyond anything I ever imagined.

We left the hotel early that night and made out way down Forty-Second Street to Times Square. I'm not sure what I expected, but it wasn't what I found. Enormous signs advertising triple X-rated shows, porn shops and clubs boasting of live sex acts were everywhere. Across the street, young women dressed in nothing but high heels and fur coats huddled together, smoking and calling to passing cars. Nothing appeared to be off-limits or unavailable.

"Prostitutes," Joey said smiling. "I wonder what I can get for a dime."

He was testing me, and I was up to the challenge. I rummaged through my purse until I found a dime.

"Here," I said handing him the coin. "Go have some fun."

I was curious as to how far he would take my dare, and watched as he turned the coin over repeatedly in his hand.

"It's tempting, but I'd hate to miss a good show."

I smiled and reached for the dime.

"Not so fast," he said grabbing my wrist. "I think I'll hold onto this. A man never knows when he might need a dime."

Joey was spontaneous and endearing, and my feelings for him grew more intense each day. Unlike Rick, who was quiet and introspective, Joey was gregarious and had a way of making everyone around him happy. His smile was contagious, and his sharp sense of humor kept me laughing. We took advantage of every opportunity to be together, but even when we weren't, I was thinking of him. I didn't want to betray Rick, so I hid my feelings behind a facade of friendship and hoped they would fade. However, I discovered suppressing emotions only fuels them, and just being in Joey's presence made my heart race.

Saturday night arrived and brought with it our first chance to navigate the city unsupervised. We had tickets to Radio City Music Hall to watch the Rockettes perform and then attend the premiere of a new movie called *Love Story*.

"Is everyone ready for a night on the town?" I quipped.

"I'm starving," Joey said. "Let's find somewhere good to eat."

I had to be careful about my spending. Earlier in the day, I calculated I had less than five dollars to spend on dinner. Finding something good to eat at that price would require a Herculean effort.

We set off in the direction of Radio City, hoping to find a spot to eat along the way. We passed plenty of restaurants, but they were all too expensive for our small budgets. As we turned yet another corner, I noticed a sign that read, "Steak, baked potato and salad: $4.95."

"What about this place?" I asked.

We peered into the cavernous restaurant and saw it was empty except for a few scruffy customers sitting at the bar.

"I don't like the look of this place. It's creepy," Kara grimaced.

"I don't like it either, but if we want to eat, it's here or nowhere."

I took a deep breath and opened the door.

"Yeah?" someone snapped.

"Table for six, please?"

"Sit anywhere ya want."

We selected the table closest to the door. I set my purse down and realized it was stuck. I pulled it off and cautioned everyone.

Several minutes later, a server approached our table. She had the reddest hair I had ever seen. Actually, it was more orange than red. She wore long, false eyelashes and even longer red nails. She studied our group and rolled her eyes. Apparently, she didn't appreciate our appearance any more than we did hers.

"What ya having?" she said, flipping open her order pad.

"I'll have the steak, cooked well-done, please," Kara said.

"We only cook 'em one way. Medium. Do ya want medium?"

Kara looked frightened, so I spoke up.

"We'll each have the steak special. Medium is fine."

The server shrugged her shoulders and vanished through the swinging door of the kitchen.

"She's rude," whispered Kara.

Kara was used to proper etiquette and genteel comportment. Adjusting to the curtness of the city was difficult for her.

"I don't think she means to be rude. People in the northeast are just different," I said.

We finished dinner and asked for our checks. Our server returned with a single check and tossed it on the table.

"Ya only get one check. Work it out amongst ya."

Someone calculated each person's share, and we laid our money on the table.

"What about the tip?" Kara asked.

"The tip? Are you kidding? They should pay us for eating in this filthy place," Joey said.

"We have to leave a tip. All the tour books say to leave at least 10% of the check."

"I don't have another dime," someone remarked.

"Just leave what you can," I suggested.

Pennies, nickels and dimes appeared from everywhere, and someone piled them in the center of the table.

"I think we'd better go," I whispered.

We raced for the door, but we weren't fast enough. Our server looked at our table from across the room and hurled profanities.

"I better not catch none of ya in here again!" she yelled.

"Don't worry. You won't," shouted Joey.

We hurried down the sidewalk toward Radio City Music Hall and arrived just before the doors closed and the orchestra started its opening number.

"Thanks for taking charge back there," Joey whispered when we sat down.

"What do you mean?"

"If it weren't for you, we'd still be searching for a place to eat."

I looked at him and almost laughed. I was no leader. I could fend for myself, but I never presumed to make decisions for anyone else. It takes confidence to do something like that. I had plenty of grit but not confidence.

The orchestra played beautifully, but my thoughts kept returning to Joey's comment. He was right. Not only had I taken charge of our group, but I had also done it without any hesitancy. I wasn't only surviving New York; I was thriving. For the first time in my life, I felt emboldened.

The Rockettes were more spectacular than I imagined, and *Love Story* was as charming and bittersweet as all the reviews reported. Yet what I remember most about that night was discovering I could trust my own judgment. My self-esteem, buried under years of insecurity, started to resurface.

Joey and I started back to the hotel alone. The rest of our group went in search of ice cream, but it was cold, and the prospect of ice cream wasn't enough to entice either of us to wander around the city. As we walked along Broadway, he reached over and took hold of my hand.

"Your hand is freezing. Where are your gloves?"

"I guess they're in my room. I wish I had them with me."

"I'm glad you don't. It's not easy to come up with an excuse to hold someone's hand."

I smiled as we kept walking, but neither of us spoke. We passed a hotel a few minutes later, and Joey led me up the steps to the entrance. We took momentary advantage of a heater above the front door that was blowing warm air for the benefit of the hotel's guests.

"I thought you'd like this. I noticed it when I was out yesterday," he said.

Joey rubbed my hands between his own until they were warm. He was unusually quiet, but I attributed his demeanor to the cold. I was wrong. He was struggling with something he wanted to say.

"Nancy, I know you're already in a relationship, and I shouldn't say this, but I have feelings for you I've never had for anyone else. I may be wrong, but I think you have feelings for me, too. Am I right?"

Joey's declaration opened a floodgate of suppressed emotions and tears ran down my face. He put his arms around me and rubbed my back.

"I didn't think you'd take it so hard," he said.

His humor helped ease the tension but only for a moment.

"You're right. I do have feelings for you, but I shouldn't. Rick trusts me, and I won't let him down.

"Is it really that easy to manipulate your feeling, or are you only fooling yourself? If you're not honest with yourself, you'll both end up hurt."

The faith I once had in my relationship with Rick was gone. I knew there were no guarantees in life, but I had been so certain. It was frightening to have doubts.

"If I give you my heart, I want to know you're prepared to give me yours. I don't need an answer now, but promise me you'll think about what I said. I need to know whether you're willing to give us a chance," Joey said.

He took my face in his hands, and although I knew I was crossing a line I couldn't step back over, I didn't move. When he kissed me, I thought of Rick and wanted to cry.

It was late when I got back to my room. Kara was asleep, and I undressed in the dark so I wouldn't wake her. She had become a trusted friend, but I wasn't prepared to talk about feelings I didn't understand. I crawled in bed, burrowed down in my covers and tried to think. I had decisions to make and actions to justify, but I was exhausted. I closed my eyes and fell asleep.

GREENWICH VILLAGE REVELATIONS 7

The next morning we learned several U.S. military units were withdrawing from Vietnam. No one knew what it meant or why it was happening, but I wondered if it might be an attempt by Nixon to appease war protesters. In spite of his November 3, televised plea for support from the "great silent majority," by 1971, fewer and fewer American's were buying into Nixon's Vietnam strategy. The previous fall, 250,000 people had descended on Washington, D. C. to participate in the largest anti-war protest in U. S. history.

That evening, Peter surprised us with an announcement that we would be going to Greenwich Village the next night for dinner and a special program. During the war, the Village was legendary for fostering individualism, freedom of expression and objection to the status quo. There was no place like it, and tomorrow night I would have the opportunity to experience it first-hand. We asked numerous questions, but Peter was unusually vague.

"Tomorrow night could have a profound effect on some of you. You'll hear things you may not agree with, but I hope you'll keep an open mind. Don't be afraid to have your convictions challenged."

Peter's comments were intriguing, but I was sure of my beliefs. At least I thought I was until the following night when they imploded, and I learned how naïve I was.

The next afternoon, we gathered at the Forty-Second Street subway station to make the trip downtown. As I descended the stairs, I encountered a heart-wrenching scene. Disheveled men and women, using over-stuffed bags to cushion their heads, lay on the few benches along the platform. Those not fortunate enough to find an empty bench simply spread out on the floor and covered their bodies with their belongings. Water dripped from overhead pipes and left a dank, musty smell circulating through the tunnel. I looked down and caught sight of a large rat running across the tracks. The city was in extreme financial distress. There was barely enough money to keep the subways running. Much less, maintain clean stations. I stood near the edge of the platform and searched the tunnel for sight of the next train.

Seconds later, a downtown train screeched to a halt, and the doors flew open. Joey grabbed my hand and ushered me to a nearby seat. In those days, the New York subways were notoriously unsafe. They served as sanctuaries for drug dealers and addicts - not to mention prostitutes, con artists and flashers. As our train gained momentum, we paid attention and watched each other's backs.

When we reached our destination, the crowd inside the station made it almost impossible to exit the train. I gripped Joey's hand as we pushed, pulled and jabbed our way up the steps. When we finally surfaced, the scene that greeted us defied description. People of every sort filled the sidewalks and spilled into the streets. Those were the days of the hippy, the flower child, war protesters, love-ins, long hair and psychedelic drugs. You didn't need to travel far from the corner of West Fourth Street and Sixth Avenue to find them all.

We maneuvered our way through the crowds to a small Italian restaurant on Sullivan Street that served pizzas cooked in wood-fired ovens.

The red and white checkered cloths on the table created a charming ambiance, but the scene outside the window was what captured our attention.

After dinner, we followed Peter to an old stone church. In spite of its blackened facade and broken stained glass windows, I thought it stood proudly in that neighborhood of seekers and sojourners. It was a survivor, and that was enough to make it a symbol of hope in those turbulent times.

The iron fence surrounding the church had rusted, and some strategically placed posts appeared to be the only thing preventing its total collapse. We passed through a gate hanging precariously from a makeshift hinge and followed Peter to a side door in the church. A few haggard men had already claimed spots in the churchyard for the night and cursed as we stepped past them. We trekked down an almost endless flight of stairs to a room that appeared to be a sort of meeting hall. Chairs were scarce, so most of us found a place on the floor to sit. I sat with my back against Joey, and he put his arms around me and rested his chin on my shoulder.

The door opened moments later, and a stranger entered. His clothes hung from a skeletal frame, and his eyes searched the room. He waved to Peter, who was making his way forward. After they spoke, the stranger took a seat in front of us.

"Welcome to New York. My name is Cody, and I'm going to spend the next couple of hours making you uncomfortable."

We smiled, but I think we were all wondering what he had in store for us.

"I'm homosexual," Cody said. "I'm not sure what that means to you, but I hope I can clear up some of the misconceptions you may have. When I finish speaking, you're free to ask me any questions you have and I promise to answer them as honestly as I can."

The silence in the room was immediate. It's doubtful any of us had ever heard someone admit to being gay. In the seventies, discrimination toward homosexuals was harsh, ugly and open. Cody was offering us extraordinary insight, and the story he shared had a profound effect on many of us, especially me.

Cody grew up in Iowa, and the night before he graduated from high school, he told his parents he was gay. His mother cried and refused to look at him. His father slapped him and said he never wanted to hear him say those words again. He got his wish. The day after graduation, Cody bought a one-way bus ticket to New York and left without saying goodbye. He had attempted to contact his parents numerous times since then, but they never responded. As far as he knew, they wanted nothing to do with him.

Eking out a living in New York was a lot harder than he expected. He slept in a youth hostel at night and worked at whatever jobs he could find. He thought his luck had turned a corner when he landed a full-time position as a bartender at a restaurant in Greenwich Village.

"Not long after I started working, I was asked to inventory the bar. The restaurant was hosting a big event later in the week, and the manager needed to order supplies the next day. I said I would take care of it before I left work.

We were busy that night, and I couldn't start on the inventory until after we closed. I was working when I heard a crash in the kitchen. Before I could reach the door, three men rushed out and grabbed me. Their faces were familiar, but I didn't know their names. I fought, but they forced me to the floor and raped me.

The next morning, the cleaning crew found me tied up and called an ambulance. I spent three days in the hospital, but I don't remember being there. The police said they would call if anything turned up, but I found out they never even went to the restaurant.

After I left the hospital, I spent the next week inside my apartment trying to decide whether to leave New York. At one point, I considered suicide. I went for a walk one day and passed Judson Memorial Church. I was tired and went inside to sit down. It wasn't long before some members of the church came over and introduced themselves. I guess they could tell something was wrong because one of them asked if I was all right. I told them my story, and they invited me to come back. It blew my mind. They were strangers, but they showed me more compassion than my own parents did. If I hadn't met them, I'm not sure I would be alive today. They gave me the support I needed to get through that crisis."

No one made a sound while Cody spoke. I think we were all trying to process what he was confiding. As for me, that run-down church in the Village was where I learned being different doesn't mean being less - it just means being different. Tolerance and respect replaced my faulty preconceived notions about homosexuality.

Not long after Cody left, the door opened again as another visitor entered the room. He looked nervous and appeared relieved when Peter stepped forward to greet him. After they spoke, the visitor took a seat in front of the room, studied our faces and began speaking.

"For purposes of confidentiality, I won't be using my real name. Just call me Michael," he said.

Michael was an American citizen living in Canada because he objected to war and refused to register for the draft. Evading the draft was one of the most controversial topics of the day. There was little sympathy for conscientious objectors and none for draft dodgers. As Michael continued speaking, there was a noticeable look of resentment on some of the faces around me.

"I moved to Canada two years ago to avoid prosecution. I'm married now and have a son. I'm here for his sake as much as mine."

Michael objected to violence and was involved in numerous underground initiatives to raise awareness about the principles of non-violent action. He had returned to the States and jeopardized his own freedom to share an alternative to war with our group and others. He met us armed only with his beliefs.

It was late when we returned to our hotel that night. I planned to go straight to bed, but when I picked up my key at the desk, the clerk handed me a message from Rick. Scribbled across the page were two words, *Call me.*

Joey was with me when I retrieved the note.

"Are you going to tell him about us?"

"I don't know what to do."

"Regardless of what you decide, someone's going to be hurt. You know that don't you?"

"That's not what I want."

"I know, but that's the way it is and you can't change it."

He turned and walked toward the elevator without looking back. I dialed Rick's number from one of the pay phones in the lobby, and he immediately answered.

"I'm sorry it's so late. We just got back to the hotel."

"It's been almost a week since I heard from you. Are you all right?"

"I'm fine."

"That's not how you sound. Why haven't you called or written?"

I paused before answering. I knew what I had to say was going to hurt Rick, but he deserved to know the truth.

"I met a boy named Joey on the Study Tour, and we've spent a lot of time together. I didn't write or try to call because I'm confused about my feelings - for you and for him."

The silence was palpable, and I could hear the disappointment in his voice when he finally spoke.

"Don't throw away what we have for someone you just met."

"I can't talk about it now. It's too hard. We can talk when I get home."

"All right, but in the meantime, there's something I want you to remember. We have a special relationship. A love like ours doesn't come along often. Don't throw it away unless you're sure everything between us is over."

A few minutes later, we said goodbye. I knew Rick was hurt and it would take a long time for the wound to heal, but it was a relief to have everything out in the open. Our relationship was built on trust, not secrecy or lies. I took the elevator to Joey's floor. It was time to be honest with everyone.

I knocked on the door twice before Joey opened it. When he did, he was wearing nothing but a towel around his waist.

"I'm sorry. I should have phoned before I came up. Were you in the shower?"

"No, I was trying out the latest fashion in cotton towel attire. What do you think of this?"

I shook my head as he proceeded to model it for me.

"I know it's late, but could you get dressed so we can go somewhere and talk?"

"Sure. I'll just be a minute. You can wait in here."

I stepped inside and was surprised to find no one else there.

"Where's Jay?"

"His uncle picked him up earlier. He lives just outside the city, and Peter let Jay and a couple of the guys go out there for the night. They'll be back tomorrow."

Joey walked out of the bathroom wearing a pair of khaki slacks and drying his hair with a towel.

"Why didn't you go with them?"

"Because I wanted to be with you."

I don't recall who moved toward the other first, but I know we both felt the same longing.

I tried to tell him we needed to talk and that I had something important to say, but then his mouth covered mine, and within minutes we were lying together on his bed. I looked in his eyes and saw tears.

"Why are there tears in your eyes?"

"I thought you were leaving me and when we got home, I'd never see you again. I swear you'll never regret this."

He was right. I never did. But, he did, and there would be times when he hated me for it, cursed the day we met, and accuse me of ruining his life. He had a right to feel that way. He thought my actions were a sign of commitment, but they weren't. As I lay in his arms, all I wanted was to love him.

Joey looked in my eyes and smiled, "I knew the first day we met we belonged together."

The spell broke and the reality of the moment left me feeling sick.

"Joey, you don't understand."

"Understand what?"

I turned my head to avoid his eyes, but he took his hand and turned my face toward his.

"You said you had something important to tell me."

"After you came upstairs, I called Rick. He could tell something was wrong, so I told him about us."

"What did he say?"

"He told me not to throw our relationship away unless I was sure everything I felt for him was over."

"And is it?"

"When we're together, I feel like it is."

"That's not what I asked."

"It's not as simple as yes or no."

"You're going back to him? Is that what you're trying to say?"

"I'm trying to say I love you, but I've felt like this before and still ended up hurt and alone."

"So you're willing to settle for someone who makes you feel safe rather than be with someone you love?"

"But, I do love him. I love you both."

He rolled over and sat on the side of the bed with his back toward me. I touched his arm, but he pushed my hand away.

"I think you'd better go."

I dried my eyes and went in the bathroom. When I came out, he was gone.

MY WORLD, HIS WORLD, ANOTHER WORLD

8

Our last day in New York finally arrived along with our last night before starting the journey home. I entered the lobby that evening and found Joey standing by the front door.

"Let's go for a walk," he said.

It was cold outside, and I shivered every time the wind blew. We stopped at the first bench we passed, and he rubbed my hands until they were warm.

"You never remember your gloves. How will you get along without me?"

He looked at my hands, and I studied his face. He was saying good-bye. I took a deep breath and tried to hold back the tears filling my eyes, but when he put his arm around me, I lay my head on his shoulder and cried.

"Please don't cry. This is my fault. I'm responsible for everything that's happened. I knew you were in a relationship, but I wouldn't accept it."

"You're wrong. I let the feelings between us grow because I wanted to be with you."

After that, there was only silence, and I stayed wrapped in his arms until the cold became unbearable. When I stood up to leave, he reached for my hand.

"I don't understand why it has to be this way."

I sat down and looked in his eyes. They were full of questions begging for answers. I had seen that look in my own eyes a thousand times and I had to help him understand.

"I was only sixteen when I met Rick, but I didn't believe in anything or anyone. Nothing mattered to me— myself least of all—but he refused to give up on me or allow me to give up on myself. He asked me to trust him, and I did. He's the only person I've ever trusted with my feelings that didn't let me down.

You were right when you said someone was going to be hurt no matter what I decided. I thought I could keep that from happening, but when I was talking to Rick last night, I realized I couldn't. I don't want to lose you, but I couldn't stand to be hurt again. I can't leave Rick."

I waited for him to say something, and when he didn't, I left. I learned the next day that he didn't go back to his room that night. His friends said he came in around dawn and refused to talk about where he'd been.

I woke up the next morning and watched as the sunlight slipped through the blinds and created shadows on the wall beside me. On the street below, car horns and delivery trucks announced the arrival of a new day. I lay in bed trying to memorize everything – every sight, sound and smell. Tomorrow morning, just like today, buses would follow their familiar routes, street vendors would serve hot coffee from makeshift carts, the *Times* would be for sale on every corner and shop owners would hose down the sidewalk in front of their stores. The rhythm of the city wouldn't miss a beat, but I would no longer be here. It was time to leave New York.

Kara stirred. We were due in the lobby at eight o'clock to start the journey home. There were bags to pack, beds to look under, and drawers to check. We would leave nothing behind – no visible sign we had ever been here.

Several hours later, we gathered our bags and took one last look around. We were almost out the door when I stopped.

"I forgot to check the bathroom. I'll meet you downstairs."

Kara smiled and hugged me tightly. She saw right through my flimsy excuse.

"Don't be too long," she said.

I went to the window and looked out at the skyline. I came to New York in search of excitement and a short reprieve from life in a small town. I found what I was seeking, but more importantly, I discovered a vast, brilliant world waiting for exploration. It was a world that challenged everything I ever believed, and I wondered if I would ever be certain of anything again. New York gave me an unquenchable thirst to learn and experience life in all its dimensions, and I knew I would never be completely content anywhere else.

I couldn't delay my departure any longer. I started to close the window but then stopped, stuck my head out and yelled, "I love you, New York, and I'll be back one day!"

"Shut up!" someone shouted from another window.

I had to laugh. It was so New York. I took one last look, lowered the window and left the room.

We're home," Joey whispered.

I opened my eyes and tried to adjust to the light inside the bus. I lifted my head from his shoulder and scanned the parking lot. It only took a moment to spot Rick standing next to his car. When I phoned that morning to ask if he would pick me up, I told him I had ended my relationship with Joey.

"Is it finished forever or just for now?"

"If you need promises, I can't make them. I'm not certain of anything anymore. All I know is that when it came time to make a choice, I knew if I left I would spend the rest of my life looking over my shoulder for you."

"I'll see you tonight," he said.

I looked at Joey. Although we held hands during the entire trip, the distance between us had grown with each mile. In a few minutes, it would be time to say goodbye.

"Rick is here to pick me up."

He turned and looked at me.

"Are you sure you want to write?"

"I'm sure."

"Then I'll write to you in a few days."

While luggage was removed from overhead, and friends said goodbye to one another, we sat looking in each other's eyes.

"Joey?"

He put his arms around me and held his face against mine. He hadn't shaved in several days and his beard pricked my skin.

"Stay with me," he whispered.

"I can't."

I closed my eyes and tried to remember everything about him. I wanted every detail seared in my mind forever.

"I should go," he said.

He stood up and grabbed his bag. I panicked when I realized he was walking away. I couldn't let him go. When would I see him again? *Would* I see him again?

"Wait!" I shouted.

He turned and came back down the aisle. When he reached me, I handed him my gloves.

"Keep these for me. If I ever need them, I'll know where they are."

He looked down at the gloves in his hand and I watched the corners of his mouth turn up.

"I might as well hold onto them. They never did you much good."

"Only when I forgot to wear them."

He looked in my eyes one last time, stuffed the gloves in his pocket and left the bus. I watched him from the window as he retrieved his bag. He had almost disappeared in the crowd when he stopped and turned toward the bus. I thought he was coming back, but then he turned and walked away. In my mind, he will always be that eighteen-year-old boy with long brown hair and an infectious smile.

When I stepped off the bus, Rick was there to take my bag.

"Was that him?"

"Yes, but I don't want to talk about him right now."

"All right, but there's one question I have to ask, and I want you to be honest. Did you come back because it's what you want or because it's what you thought you should do?"

I looked in his face, but he was guarding his emotions. I knew he was hurt, but he would never allow himself to show it.

"The truth is I need someone who believes in me and won't walk away . . . no matter what."

I knew he was struggling with his feelings, but even so, a slight smile spread across his face and he put his arm around my shoulder. When we got to his car, he put my bag in the trunk and then opened my door. I was about to sit down when I stopped and turned toward him.

"It's all right to say you're glad I'm home. It doesn't mean you forgive me."

"I'm glad you're home. It wasn't easy being apart."

His kiss was slow, tender and full of understanding. Despite the fact he had every right to be angry, he wasn't. At that moment, I understood what attracted me to both Rick and Joey. Rick's devotion and unconditional love gave me the sense of security I needed but had never known. Joey's exuberance and passion for life made me feel alive. I needed all those qualities, but I hadn't found them in one person. I'd found them in two.

Rick was about to start the car, but I stopped him.

"There's something I need to tell you."

"No, there isn't. There's nothing you need to tell me."

We looked at each other for a long time without speaking.

"Let's go home," he said.

I was exhausted from the long bus ride, and as we pulled out of the parking lot, I rested my head against his shoulder. I knew I was lucky he still cared. Sometimes I felt as if he knew me better than I knew myself. Maybe that's what helped him forgive my mistakes and blunders.

As we turned onto the highway and Rick's car picked up speed, my thoughts turned to Joey. The memory of him looking back at the bus troubled me. Was there something else he wanted to say? Would I ever know? I knew staying with Rick was the right decision, but I also knew it would take a long time to put aside my feelings for Joey. I already missed him.

I closed my eyes and let scenes of New York flow through my mind. My experience taught me a great deal about the world and even more about myself. I was a girl from a small town, but I wasn't a small-town girl. The life I wanted didn't exist in small places. I also knew that wherever life took me, I wanted Rick by my side. We might never satisfy all of each other's needs, but together we were better than either of us was apart. I reached for his hand, and it was there.

A FRESH START

9

"It was the best of times, it was the worst of times, it was the age of wisdom, it was the age of foolishness . . ."

Charles Dickens's famous words were barely out of Marsolete's mouth when someone knocked on our door. She groaned and heaved her stout body from her chair. My English teacher despised class interruptions almost as much as she hated leaving her seat.

The messenger at the door handed Marsolete a note. She read it, glared over the rim of her glasses and told me to report to the office. Report to the office? But, why? I hadn't done anything – at least nothing I could remember.

Big Tom wasn't in his office, so I began considering my options. If I left before he returned, he might get busy and forget whatever transgression I'd committed. On the other hand, if he did remember, I could truthfully say I went to his office, but no one was there.

"You can wait inside," his secretary called from across the room. "He's expecting you."

I reluctantly abandoned my scheming and took a seat in Big Tom's office. A few minutes later, he entered the room and dropped into his chair.

"Sorry to keep you waiting. It's been like a zoo around here today."

"I can explain," I said.

"Explain what?"

"What I did."

"What did you do?"

"I'm not sure."

"Did I miss something? What are we talking about?"

"Well, you sent for me, didn't you?"

Big Tom leaned back in his chair and laughed, "You can relax. You're not in trouble. You won the Civitan Scholarship. I got the call this morning but I've been too busy to tell you."

I stared at Big Tom and waited for him to say "Gotcha," but he didn't. He was serious.

"It covers the entire cost of an undergraduate degree. I wish I could see your mother's face when you give her the news."

"Why would they give it to me?"

"They didn't say, but it could be for any number of reasons. I will admit I sometimes doubted I would ever have a conversation like this with you, but I couldn't be happier."

I didn't know what to ask or even say. Big Tom stared at me a moment then turned to some paper work. Was he finished? Should I leave?

"Do you know much about horse racing?" he asked.

What did horse racing have to do with anything?

"Bets are placed according to a particular horse's chance of winning a race. Do you understand?"

I nodded my head in spite of the fact I was convinced his years as a high school principal had finally driven him mad.

"Think of it this way. Someone examined the odds and decided you were worth the gamble. They have confidence in you or they wouldn't have made the bet."

During high school, I gave Big Tom plenty of reasons to toss me to the dogs, but he didn't. His support was always there for me. I threw my arms around his broad shoulders and hugged him.

"If you hadn't placed a stake in my future a long time ago, no one would be gambling on it now."

"Chances like this don't come along often. Remember that."

Before I walked out the door, I turned and looked at him one last time.

"I know you have a million reasons not to trust anything I say, but I won't let you down."

Big Tom winked and went back to his paperwork. It was his way of saying he trusted me, and I wouldn't have traded it for a thousand scholarships.

Austin Peay State University offered the type of personal, academic experience for which I was looking. Furthermore, it gave me a chance to be near Rick, who decided Austin Peay was also the perfect college for him. However, it's possible he just wanted to keep an eye on me.

Classes didn't begin until late August, so I looked for a summer job. After six years as a babysitter, I had to be qualified for something more professional. When a local department store offered me a sales position in women's fashions, I jumped at the chance.

I arrived at the store eager to begin my new line of work, but unfortunately, my enthusiasm was short-lived. The clothes sold by our store were some of the most poorly constructed I had ever seen. I felt an obligation to help my customers make good decisions, but I soon learned that honesty wasn't a quality held in high regard by Ms. Pennington, the manager of women's fashions.

"I love it! This is exactly what I was looking for. What do you think?"

I stared at my customer's reflection in the mirror and frowned. The short, stocky blonde standing in front of me and waiting for approval was dressed in a suit from our new fall collection. She had somehow managed to squeeze her size 14 body into a size 8 skirt, but it looked awful. Fortunately, there were so many flaws in the actual suit, it wouldn't be necessary to address the size.

"It is a beautiful color, but the buttons aren't lined up properly, and one side of the collar looks shorter than the other."

My customer was scrutinizing the suit in a nearby mirror, when Ms. Pennington suddenly appeared.

"Please excuse us. Your sales associate will be with you again in just a moment,"

Pennington grabbed my arm and led me aside.

"What the hell do you think you're doing?"

"Trying to make sure my customer is satisfied with her purchase. I know the store's reputation is important."

"Your job is selling clothes, not safeguarding the store's reputation. That's my business, and I don't need help doing it."

Pennington's reprimands were unpleasant, but they didn't begin to compare to the disgusting dose of sexual harassment offered by the Assistant Store Manager, Mr. Boyle. Earlier in the day, I was dressing a mannequin when he wandered over to offer his self-styled assistance.

"See how easy it is. You just push this stick in the hole between her legs," he said.

Boyle infuriated me. He used his position to harass everyone he supervised and it had to stop. No one should have to tolerate that type of behavior.

Rick picked me up from work that night, and by the time I finished telling him about Boyle, he was seething.

"He's a jerk. Do you want me to talk to him? I guarantee he won't bother you again."

"Thanks, but this is my problem and I think I should be the one to handle it."

The next day, I requested a meeting with the manager of the store. I had met Mr. Crowley on several occasions, and he had always been cordial.

"Please have a seat," he said as I entered his office. "I understand this is about Mr. Boyle."

Poor Mr. Crowley. As I launched into my account of Boyle's deplorable behavior, his eyes grew large and he leaned forward in his chair. When I finished speaking, there was a knock on the door and his assistant entered.

"Mr. Crowley, I thought you'd like to know there are other employees waiting to speak with you about Mr. Boyle."

The door opened, and at least a dozen oppressed female associates marched into Mr. Crowley's office and unleashed their collective fury. I had a feeling Mr. Crowley's assistant had a big mouth.

When our meeting ended, I went back to work and arrived just in time to hear Pennington assisting a customer.

"This dress is made for you, and you won't find it in any other store."

She was probably right. No store but ours would have the nerve to sell a dress that was two inches shorter in the back than it was in the front.

The following day, a memo informed us that Mr. Boyle had decided to seek other employment opportunities. Morale improved but not for long. A week later, Ms. Pennington was promoted to Assistant Manager. She was smiling when she reassigned me to the least desirable department in the entire store – the cosmetics department.

Life behind the makeup counter was equivalent to death-by-boredom. I spent my days in the mindless pursuit of organizing seldom-used products and reading the outrageous claims on their packaging. One bottle of spray cologne claimed to provide *instant freshness and a sense of well-being*. If all it took to maintain a sense of well-being was a whiff of that cologne, I had a feeling we would sell out of it faster than we could stock it.

When I was unable to escape Pennington's attention, I performed the unthinkable and manipulated decent people into buying products they didn't need at prices they couldn't afford. Cajole, deceive, fleece – I don't know how I lived with myself after perpetrating such deception.

Summer ended and so did my days at the department store. I wasn't cut out for the retail world, but it did teach me some valuable lessons. I learned I would rather stand up for what's right and face the consequences than let fear prevent me from speaking out. I also learned if I'm required to be dishonest, I'm probably in the wrong place and doing the wrong thing for the wrong people.

STRAIGHT PATHS   10

With my job behind me, I concentrated on selecting classes for my first semester at Austin Peay. Choosing a major was harder than I expected. My high school curriculum was regimented and dull, but the university offered limitless options.

Rick didn't struggle. He decided to major in accounting and worked out his schedule before I even finished reading the first page of the college handbook. I hoped once classes began something would grab my attention. Regardless of my dilemma, college represented a new chapter in my life, and it couldn't get here fast enough.

Although college students were eligible to defer military service until after graduation, Rick decided to take a chance in the lottery. A college deferment would only postpone the inevitable and he didn't want his future dictated by the draft . . . not if there was another option. I didn't support his decision. He knew nothing about guns or war. He was an eighteen-year-old boy who had never even been in a fight. It was impossible to imagine him dressed in mud-caked, camouflaged clothing marching through a jungle with a gun across his chest. The war was a nightmare, and I wanted it to end before it hurt anyone else I loved.

The lottery was on August 5. Depending on the outcome, Rick might be on his way to Vietnam. That night we stared at the television and held our breath as each day of the year was assigned a number from one to 365. When Rick's birthday, March 3, was drawn, the draft number was up to 170 and his chance of going to Vietnam was small. I was relieved and thankful, but far from happy. Many of our friends weren't as fortunate. They were destined to fight in a war most people no longer believed was worth fighting. They would leave and return home broken, wounded and changed forever. The war would rob them of something they could never recover – their innocence.

I checked the mail each day hoping to find Joey's familiar scrawl on an envelope. We wrote every week and shared our lives and dreams through our letters. We never touched on our feelings. It was a pledge we made due to my relationship with Rick, but also because it was too painful. When I told Rick we were writing, he was angry but tolerant.

"I'll accept it as long as this is about a friendship, but if it ever becomes more than that, we're finished for good."

I knew he was serious, and I didn't intend to jeopardize our relationship. Yet, I struggled with the unresolved emotions I felt for Joey. His undergraduate major was Religious Studies. After college, he planned to attend a divinity school or seminary. His goal was to become an ordained minister. He was the only person I ever confided in about my longing to believe in God and experience faith. He knew exactly what I meant and wanted the same thing. I was glad he was following his heart.

Registration day dawned at last. I got up early, pulled on my jeans, stuffed my head through a black turtleneck, and drove to campus. My early arrival would guarantee my enrollment in the classes I selected – at least that's what I thought. Unfortunately, my morning rush proved useless. When I reached campus, I found several hundred students standing in a line wrapped halfway around the gym. I took a spot at the end and waited. Within an hour, most of the classes I hoped to take were full, and I wondered if anything interesting would even be available by the time I reached the front of the line.

An hour later, I handed an advisor my registration package. He scrutinized every page so slowly that I wondered if the tortoise-shell glasses he wore interfered with his vision. They had the annoying habit of working their way down the bridge of his nose.

"This says you're undecided on a major. Is that true?"

I felt like I was acknowledging a crime.

"Sir, to be honest, I don't have a clue about my major."

"Jim," he said.

"Excuse me?"

"My name is Jim. Most people call me Dr. Nixon, but you can call me Jim. Just don't call me sir. It makes me feel old."

My exasperation was on the verge of morphing into despair. I was tired, confused and frustrated. All I wanted was help, not a conversation.

"Okay, Dr. Nixon, I mean, Jim, as I was saying, I don't know what my major will be, so could you just help me select some classes that will be useful in some way at some point?"

He stared at me for a moment, removed his glasses and said, "Bullshit."

"Excuse me?"

"That's bullshit, and you know it. I'm not going to let you take up space in a class that doesn't interest you. So tell me, what are you interested in learning?"

"I'm interested in lots of things, but if I had to pick just one, it would be people."

He looked at me in a peculiar sort of way.

"What is it you want to learn about people?"

"I'd like to know what makes a person who they are."

"Would you be interested in finding out what makes a society act the way it does? Study current problems faced by people living in urban environments or research ethnic relations?"

"Is that a major?"

"Indeed, it is. It's called sociology, and I think you should give it a try."

He was right. The study of sociology satisfied the intellectual void I had felt since leaving New York. Over the course of my first year in college, Jim became my mentor and friend. He introduced me to social inequality, social psychology, Karl Marx, Margaret Mead and Robert Merton. While taking his course "Crime and Delinquency," I discovered that during my adolescence, I possessed eight out of ten known risk factors linked to a life of crime. By all rights, I should be writing this book from prison.

Jim arrived on campus just a few days before me. He left the University of Michigan to become Chairman of Austin Peay's Sociology Department. I found his personal story fascinating. He was an ordained minister who left the church because he believed he could have a more powerful and direct impact without its constraints. He opposed the war and helped organize an underground movement against it. His intellect, compassion and fierce dedication to his beliefs inspired and challenged me. He continued my education that began one evening in the basement of a run-down church in Greenwich Village.

My first term paper in sociology was about the fatal shooting at Kent State of four unarmed students who were protesting the war in Vietnam. The killings sparked protests throughout the entire nation. By the fall of 1971, the anti-war movement was in full swing. Polls showed less than half the country supported military action in Vietnam, but I didn't need to hear the numbers. All I had to do was look at the signs around campus to know where people stood.

When my second year of college began, we were still engrossed in the war. Month after month, bodies came home, tears fell and demonstrations occurred. Like everyone else, I dreamed of an end to the violence.

On the night of January 23, 1973, I was lying in bed reading when I heard President Nixon's voice on the radio.

"I have asked for this radio and television time tonight for the purpose of announcing that we today have concluded an agreement to end the war and bring peace with honor to Vietnam and in Southeast Asia."

I stared at the radio. Did Nixon just say the war was over? I called Rick. He also heard the announcement. It was true. The war was over, but it was years too late. Millions of lives had been shattered and lost. I looked at the silver POW bracelet on my left wrist and ran my finger across the name engraved on it. I had worn it for the past two years as a visible sign I cared about the men and women fighting in the war. I never learned if the soldier named on my bracelet returned home, but I prayed he did.

I went to the mailbox one afternoon and found a letter from Joey. I was surprised because it had been less than a week since his last letter. I took it to my room and lay down on my bed.

"This will be my last letter and it's important to me that you understand why. I thought we could just be friends, but I was wrong. I can't go from loving you to simply liking you. I wish I could change how I feel, but I can't. I miss you all the time, and I wonder if you ever miss me. I know it's wrong, but there's a part of me that hopes you hurt at least as much as I do."

Tears fell from my eyes and it was difficult to breathe. I knew this letter would arrive one day. It was inevitable. I never gave Joey any hope of our being together again. Yet, if I were honest with myself, neither had I done anything to discourage him. Our letters were the only way I had of holding a place in his heart, and I had selfishly taken advantage of it.

I turned and stared out the window. My eyes landed on the stepping-stones in my mother's garden. I remembered the day Johnny set them in the ground, and how hard he worked to keep the path straight.

"I think paths that twist and turn are more interesting," I said.

"Maybe, but straight paths are safer."

Johnny was right. Straight paths *are* safer, but it's not in my nature to gravitate toward them. Joey is evidence of that.

I reached under my bed and pulled out a box of stationery. I chose a pale blue card and wrote a note that spoke to everything in my heart.

"Do I miss you? Does being apart hurt *me* as much as it hurts you? The answer to your first question is yes. I miss you every day we're apart. I thought in time it would get easier, but I was wrong. I don't know the answer to your second question. All I know is that a piece of my heart still belongs to you and feels like it always will. Even so, I know the decision I made was best for all of us. One day, you'll realize it, too, and understand I did this as much for you as for myself.

Try to remember the happiest moment we ever shared and let that be the memory you hold in your heart forever. It will be in mine also."

I closed my eyes and let images of Joey roll across my mind. His voice, his laugh, his hair falling across his eyes and my hand brushing it aside, his face next to mine and my hand holding his. I treasured those memories, but it was time to put them away. I placed his letter in my box of keepsakes along with all his others and closed the lid. Someday, when it stopped hurting, I knew I would read each one of them again.

BETTY CROCKER AND FRENCH BORDELLOS

11

The end of the war brought change to campus. The music of Three Dog Night, Chicago, The Eagles, and Creedence Clearwater Revival replaced news broadcasts. Pot began showing up more and more frequently at parties and streaking became the craze. On any given night, weather permitting, hundreds of students would gather to watch for *the streaker*. He would appear out of nowhere and run buck-naked across campus with the police in hot pursuit. A sighting generated applause worthy of a skilled athlete.

With the weight of the war removed from our shoulders, college became fun. Rick and I played tennis, went to parties, danced, and cheered for our teams. We were in that wonderful sheltered space that exist between adolescence and adulthood, and would probably have stayed longer, except everyone we knew was either engaged or getting married. Even Linda returned home one night with a ring on her finger.

Rick agreed we should get married, but our timelines differed. I saw no reason to delay, but he had a different idea. Whenever I broached the subject, he always gave the same response:

"I'm not getting married until I graduate from college and know I can support a family."

Money was a serious issue to Rick. Although both his parents worked hard, they struggled to make ends meet. He grew up listening to them quarrel over money, and he was determined not to let the same thing happen in his own marriage.

"You can wait as long as you want, but don't assume I'll be available," I would retort.

"I guess that's just a chance I'll have to take," he'd say.

I have no doubt Rick meant what he said, but he later decided it wasn't a chance he was willing to take after all. Instead of waiting until after graduation, he asked me to marry him the summer before our senior year. It was not a hasty decision; he never took any decision lightly. For months, he analyzed marriage from every angle and didn't propose until he was convinced we could survive on our combined part-time salaries of eighty-five dollars a week.

We married on a Sunday afternoon in August. I carried a bouquet of daisies as I walked down the aisle with Johnny. He went by *John* now, but he would always be *Johnny* to me.

When we reached the end of the aisle, we stopped so I could hand my mother a daisy from my bouquet. Our eyes connected for only a moment, but it was long enough to expose her emotions. She smiled in spite of the tears falling from her eyes. She had worked so hard and so long on my behalf. Had I ever told her she was the finest mother anyone could ever have?

As we reached the altar of the church, Johnny placed my hand in Rick's. My parents' divorce taught me marriage requires commitment. Only time would tell if Rick and I cherished each other the way we should, but I knew with absolute certainty that our unlikely match had blossomed into something extraordinary. Rick trusted me, and I had learned to trust him.

The night before we married, I burned all my letters from Joey. There was no place them in my marriage. I put the ashes in an envelope and tucked it inside the suitcase I was taking on our honeymoon. We were sitting on the beach late one night when I reached in my bag and handed Rick the envelope. He opened it and looked puzzled.

"What's this?"

"Proof."

"Proof of what?"

"That you're the only one I love."

"You killed the guy and had him cremated?"

"No, just his letters."

"I didn't ask for proof."

"You never asked for anything - not details or even an explanation."

"I don't need proof. All I need is you."

He walked into the surf and threw the envelope in the water.

"Now the proof is gone," I shouted from the beach.

"No, now *he's* gone."

Our first home was in one of my mother's rental apartments. Yes, it was one of *those* apartments. We spent weeks decorating it to suit our personal taste, and each room had a different theme. The living room, with its leather furniture and tall, dark bookcases, resembled an English library.

We filled the cabinets with books bought from a quaint second-hand shop near the center of town. The fact that the books and their authors were virtually unknown was immaterial. They created an air of intellectualism, looked nice and were cheap.

Our small bedroom had the unmistakable look of a French bordello - red bed linens, red rugs, red pillows and curtains. The only thing missing was a mirror above the bed. The kitchen was straight out of the 1950s. The focal point was an old RCA Whirlpool refrigerator. For some reason, frost accumulated on every shelf. When the door was open, it was like looking into an igloo.

Across the room sat an original Maytag wringer washing machine. It came with the apartment, so Rick insisted I learn to use it. I didn't dare complain because to do so would provoke his monologue on why we should have waited until after graduation to marry. If we had waited, he reasoned, he would have a real job, and I would have a real washing machine.

The crown jewel of the apartment was our spare bedroom (a.k.a. the Tropicana.) We painted the furniture with expensive lime-green lacquer paint that dried to a slick finish and purchased a bedspread with matching curtains that displayed large cockatoos. The Tropicana was our oasis in the desert of reality.

The apartment was eclectic, bold and inviting. It was our first home, and it brought out the best in us – our best times, our best love and our best memories.

I quickly learned that compatibility isn't guaranteed just because two people are pronounced husband and wife. A happy marriage requires compromise - especially when it comes to food. I tried to serve meals Rick would enjoy, but it was a wasted effort. Every attempt I made to prepare edible fare proved disastrous. The low point of my culinary trials was the night I presented him with a dish of broccoli fritters. The recipe was from my new Betty Crocker cookbook.

When the timer went off, I carefully removed the pan from the top shelf of the oven. Flat, round green discs were floating in a sea of olive oil and garlic. How had something so vile-looking earned a spot on the pages of the most popular cookbook of its day? There was no time to prepare anything else, so I went into action and hoped for the best. I put the fritters back in the oven and closed the door.

A few minutes later, I heard Rick's car pull in the driveway. He came in the kitchen, gave me a quick kiss and sat down at the table.

"What's for dinner?"

"It's a surprise."

I took the fritters from the oven and placed them on the table. Rick stared in total silence.

"What is that?" he asked.

"Broccoli fritters, of course."

"You make it sound as if we have them every night. I've never seen anything like that."

It took less than a minute for him to speak the words I had longed to hear for months.

"Do we have any frozen TV dinners?"

"Sure! Do you want fried chicken with mashed potatoes or Salisbury steak with green beans?"

Broccoli fritters were the tipping point. Rick's surrender to prepackaged food meant there was no end to the variety of tasty meals we could enjoy. When it came to TV dinners, I was a master chef. The following day

I made a stop at our local Salvation Army Store. The woman behind the counter looked puzzled when I handed her my donation.

"Are you sure you want to give this away? It looks brand new."

I glanced down at my Betty Crocker cookbook and smiled.

"You're right. It is difficult to part with. It was a wedding gift, but in honor of my marriage I've decided to share it."

I turned and left the store before she could give it back.

Between President Nixon's resignation, the energy crisis, and failure to ratify the Equal Rights Amendment, it felt like everything was falling apart. Everything, that is, except my marriage. Even on my worst days, life with Rick was good.

As soon as we graduated, we made plans to move. Nashville wasn't far and held opportunities our small town didn't, so we set our sights on Music City. We left our lime-green furniture for the next tenants of our apartment, traded our books with the unfamiliar titles and authors for a collection of the classics, and sold the Maytag washing machine to a family who lived on the outskirts of town. They converted it to a flowerpot and set it at the end of their driveway. Sadly, the Whirlpool refrigerator had died of old age by the time we left, and red was no longer in vogue — not even in *real* French bordellos.

Nashville was the perfect place to begin a new life. Like us, it was on the move. The music industry was beginning to bypass places like New York and L.A. for studios on Nashville's Music Row. Country music was enjoying unprecedented popularity. Nashville was *hot*, and we basked in its warmth.

Rick accepted a position in the Audit Department at Vanderbilt University, and I took a job as a fourth-grade teacher in a local elementary school. Parental support was strong in those days, and collaborative efforts between home and school created an atmosphere that helped students flourish. Teaching was everything I had hoped it would be.

We purchased a small house on a quiet street and busied ourselves with creating a home we thought we would live in forever. We took disco lessons, had dinner parties, went water skiing and never, under any circumstances, missed Saturday Night Live. Those were the days of Gilda Radner, Chevy Chase, John Belushi, Jane Curtin, Dan Aykroyd, Gerald Morris and Laraine Newman. Each week when I heard "Live from New York – it's Saturday Night!" I experienced a twinge of melancholy. Otherwise, I was content on all levels. We were young and happy. We had settled in and settled down. Life had fallen into a comfortable, predictable pattern that suited us well. We were free to invent our own destiny and write our own story. The possibilities were endless – for almost six years.

I opened my eyes and looked at the clock. It was only seven a.m., but Rick was already gone. He was spending far too many hours at work these days.

The moment I sat up, a queasy feeling sent me running to the bathroom. I hung my head over the toilet and heaved. This dreadful nausea was becoming more and more frequent. The day before, I barely had time to pull the car off the road before getting sick. I was suspicious of the cause and wondered if I should purchase one of the new home pregnancy tests available at the drug store. I hesitated only because I was sure it was a false alarm.

I couldn't be pregnant . . . could I? Then again, I didn't recall having a period since our trip to Atlanta in early March to celebrate Rick's 27th birthday. Our destination was Underground Atlanta – an underground mall of nightclubs, restaurants and awesome music venues. We danced until morning and ended the evening harmonizing on *A Rainy Night in Georgia.* Actually, singing wasn't quite how the evening ended, and that's what had me worried.

Later in the day, I showered, dressed and headed for the drug store. In those days, women's personal products were a private matter. I was too embarrassed to ask for a pregnancy test, so my only option was to browse the entire store. I found everything *but* the tests. Left with no alternative, I approached the clerk at the checkout counter.

"The what?" asked the girl.

"You know," I whispered, "those new tests that show if a person is pregnant."

"Oh, *those* tests."

I watched in horror as she picked up a small microphone that fed into a loud speaker.

"Dr. Davis, do we still have any home pregnancy tests?" she asked.

The sound shattered the silence, and everyone stared in our direction. I dropped my head in shame and wished I could disappear.

"They're back here," he shouted.

"They're back at the pharmacy desk," the clerk said.

I studied her face and wondered how anyone could be so void of social judgment. I tried to clear my thoughts and focus on my current predicament. I couldn't walk past all those staring eyes, but I needed one of those tests.

"I'm sorry to bother you, but I'm not feeling well. Would you mind getting one of the tests for me?" I asked the clerk.

"Are you all right? Do you want me to get Dr. Davis?"

"Oh no, I'll be fine. I just need to go home and lie down."

She made her way around the counter and headed for the back of the store. When she returned, I paid her for the test and fled the store. As I started my car and headed for home, I weighed the consequences of that rainy night in Georgia.

Rick and I had discussed having a baby in the future, but not now, not when everything was so ominous. The current recession was lasting longer than anyone had anticipated. Who knew when it would end? We could lose our jobs, our home or even our life savings. In addition, there was political unrest abroad and worldwide ecological concerns. Smog was killing people, the polar ice cap was melting and there was the possibility of a nuclear holocaust. Why would any sane person choose to bring a helpless baby into such a threatening environment?

Nonetheless, when the results of my pregnancy test came back positive, we were ecstatic. Suddenly, the economy gained steam, and problems abroad weren't so intimidating. The polar ice cap? No one knew for certain if it was melting. Nuclear annihilation? Negotiations were going on all the time. We were having a baby, and just like magic, everything was perfect.

We wasted no time preparing for our baby. We sold the office furniture in our spare bedroom to make room for the white crib we purchased at a yard sale. Rick painted the nursery a soft shade of yellow, and I made a blue and white canopy to hang over the bed. We purchased a rocking chair, a Beatrix Potter wind-up mobile that played *Here Comes Peter Cottontail*, folded diapers and got out the baby wipes. We were prepared for everything. Everything, except the one thing no one ever expected to happen: my father was coming to town, and he wanted to see me.

EXPLANATIONS, HEALING AND LOVE 12

"Daddy loves you."

Those were my father's last words before he turned and walked out of my life forever. What kind of love is that? The kind that shatters lives and destroys trust. My father was good at both.

The days leading up to his visit were difficult. I was anxious and troubled by the prospect of seeing my father again. If there was a particular reason for his trip, he did not share it. My delivery date was in less than four weeks, and nothing short of a visit to my doctor would ease Rick's concern for me.

The night before our scheduled meeting, I went to bed early but found sleep impossible. I lay awake envisioning disturbing scenes and ugly accusations. It was almost morning before I managed to doze.

"Nancy, it's time to get up. You have to be at Linda's soon."

I opened my eyes and found Rick sitting next to me on our bed.

"I waited as late as possible before waking you. I don't think you went to sleep until after three o'clock. Are you sure, you want to put yourself through this? You don't have to go. I could call and tell them you're not feeling well."

I looked at Rick's anxious face and placed his hand on my stomach.

"You don't need to worry. I'll be fine."

A second later, he felt a hard kick and smiled. He loved feeling the baby move.

"Are you going to kick for your grandfather?" he asked the bulge protruding from underneath my gown.

My smile turned into an angry scowl and I turned my face away.

"I wish you wouldn't say things like that. He wasn't a father to me and he won't be a grandfather to our child."

I tried sitting up, but like a beached whale, my weight made it impossible.

"Will you help me up so I can get ready? I have a long drive ahead."

"You're not driving. I am."

"No. We've already discussed this. I don't want you to come. I want to do this on my own."

"You've had almost no sleep. I'm coming with you whether you agree or not. The timing of your father's visit couldn't be worse. The most important thing to consider is your health and our baby. You can be obstinate some other time, but not today. Today, you're in my hands."

I saw the determination in his eyes and knew he intended to win this battle.

"Considering the fact I'm carrying thirty extra pounds around my waist and can barely squeeze behind the steering wheel of our car, I'll yield to your bullying, but only this once."

"I swear I'll never bully you again."

He bent down to kiss me, but I raised my hand.

"No one likes a bully."

"I'll remember that," he said.

Why was my father here? What possible reason could he have for coming, and why now? Why had he waited so many years to return?

We decided our visit would take place at Linda's home. Everyone would be there except Johnny. He wanted no part of our so-called reunion. He had no respect for our father and refused to acknowledge him.

When we reached Linda's, I was surprised to find my father's car already parked in front of her house. My heart started racing. I thought we would arrive long before him. I planned to have time to prepare myself. Rick saw the panic on my face and reached for my hand.

"Remember, we can leave whenever you're ready."

He helped me out of the car and to the front door. My apprehension was overwhelming, but my curiosity was even greater. Would I recognize him? Would he recognize me? I braced myself and knocked. Linda answered the door, and we followed her to the living room. The moment we entered, my father stepped forward to greet us.

"This is Nancy and her husband, Rick," said my mother.

It was a moment I had envisioned a thousand times, yet the reality was starkly different from my dreams. The man I once called *Daddy* abandoned our relationship years ago, and now we were strangers. The fact that we required an introduction tore at my heart.

As I stood facing my father, years of unrealized dreams crumbled and landed at my feet. I was devastated by something I thought I had accepted years ago – I was never going to have a father. How could I have been so naïve? I was astonished at my stupidity. The realization that my dreams – dreams I had never shared with anyone – were nothing but a fantasy hurt more than I can express.

The conversation was absurd. Was the traffic bad? Were the directions good? How long will you be here? I felt like screaming. Surely, there were more important things to discuss.

My father eventually turned to my mother and began reminiscing about their past. Did she remember the time they went fishing and turned over in the boat? What about the pet shop she opened before the children came along? Did she recall the trouble they had finding homes for all the animals when she decided to stop working? Did she remember how Nancy cried when they brought John home from the hospital?

The cruelty of his recollections was lost on him but not on Linda. It was more than she could bear, and she left the room crying. Given the circumstances, I thought my mother displayed remarkable composure. I wondered more than once if my father's request to see his children was really an excuse to see her.

I waited for my father to acknowledge all the years he had been away, but he did not. He spoke as if those years never existed. I spent most of them believing he left because I wasn't good enough. My mother spent them working day and night to care for our family. My father's absence demanded an explanation, but he offered none. For me, that was the most heart-breaking part of his visit.

I glanced at Rick and wasn't surprised to find him looking at me. As always, he was guarding my well-being. I looked from him to my father; from a man who gave me unconditional love, to a man who offered me no love at all; from the person who had salvaged my self-esteem, to the person who had crushed it.

I couldn't tolerate being there any longer and invented an excuse to leave early. I gathered my coat and purse and said goodbye. My father followed me out of the room, and when we reached the front door, I turned and extended my hand. It was a cruel gesture, and I hoped it would wound him as much as his last embrace haunted me.

I was only a child then, a girl who curled her hair and wore her father's favorite dress to please him. I mistook his laughter and the way he picked me up and twirled me around to mean he cared, but I was wrong. Today, unlike before, I had no illusions. My father's visit changed nothing. My hope of explanations, healing and love vanished, and I left with the same empty place in my heart with which I had arrived.

LIFE AND DEATH 13

Four weeks later, I was too busy to give my father's visit a second thought. Following a momentary pause to show me the tiny infant who had just slipped from my body, the doctor rushed across the room and placed her face under an oxygen mask.

"She's so blue. Is she all right?" I asked.

"She's fine. She just needs some air."

After twenty-four hours of torturous labor, followed by natural childbirth, I was eager to accept his positive diagnosis. However, as he spoke, the delivery room began to take on the appearance of Grand Central Station during rush hour. My daughter disappeared behind a sea of white coats, and someone rolled my bed to another room. I later learned the umbilical cord had wrapped around her neck during labor, and as she passed through the birth canal, it tightened and shut off her access to oxygen. Fortunately, the prompt action of the delivery room staff prevented any serious complications.

We named our tiny little girl with silky auburn hair *Kathryn*. A nurse wrapped her in a soft yellow blanket and handed her to me. I knew this helpless child possessed the ability to produce enormous changes in my life; however, I hadn't realized they would begin immediately.

I tried to prepare myself for our baby's arrival. I studied how to hold, feed, bathe and play with a newborn. I stocked the nursery with recommended creams, potions, toys and equipment. I thought I was ready, but now that she was here, it didn't feel that way. I couldn't remember a single thing I had read. She was so tiny and so dependent. I was terrified I might drop her and she would break into a million pieces. When the nurse brought her to me for her first feeding, I panicked.

"Don't worry. She knows what to do," the nurse said as she turned and left the room. Her message was the totality of breastfeeding assistance given to first-time mothers of my generation. Lactation services, common in today's hospitals, weren't on the radar in 1979. I looked in my daughter's eyes, apologized for my inexperience and held her to my breast.

Two days after Kathryn's birth, we prepared to go home. While Rick went to get the car, a nurse came to my room with a wheelchair. After getting me settled, she went to retrieve my baby.

Kathryn entered the room kicking and screaming. I wondered if somehow she had figured out she was about to be parted from the safety of her hospital bed. Her cries pierced my ears and left me feeling hopelessly inadequate.

The nurse wheeled us from the room, and we made our way toward the elevator. Within minutes, we would leave the sanctuary of the hospital, and I would be responsible for this tiny infant. Why didn't someone stop us? Couldn't they see I didn't have the least idea what I was doing? Kathryn's cries grew louder and more anguished. She was obviously in distress. Why didn't someone do something? I began to panic.

"Why is she crying? What does she want?"

"Her thumb," the nurse replied.

She reached down and turned back the cuff on Kathryn's gown. Within seconds, Kathryn's thumb was in her mouth and her crying ceased. I was amazed.

"How did you know what she wanted?"

"Most babies like their thumb. If it's not that, the problem is usually a wet diaper or time to nurse."

Rick met us at the front door. He was all smiles as he took Kathryn from my arms and strapped her into her new car seat. The nurse helped me into the car and studied my worried face.

"Don't worry," she whispered. "She's a lot tougher than she looks."

She smiled and closed the door. Rick started the car and then turned toward me.

"Are you ready?" he asked.

"Of course. You just have to remember she's a lot tougher than she looks."

Rick looked bewildered. Where was the hysterical woman he had left in a hospital room barely ten minutes before? As we left the parking lot, I turned and looked at my sweet baby. You can't fool me, I thought. I know this is just a brief reprieve before the next storm, but I'm ready for you - now that I know you're a lot tougher than you look. I lay my head back on the seat, closed my eyes and slept like a baby.

Caring for a newborn was harder than I expected, but fortunately, Rick had the knack for parenting that I lacked. His calm demeanor helped soothe Kathryn and alleviate my fears . . . well, most of them. Kathryn was two weeks old when I was dressing her one morning and felt a hard lump under her left nipple. I checked the other side, but there was none. It could only mean one thing – breast cancer. I rushed to the phone and called her doctor. He was booked all day but said he would work me in as soon as possible. I grabbed Kathryn and rushed out the door.

When we arrived at the doctor's office, we were ushered into an exam room. I was explaining the situation to the nurse when the door opened and Rick entered. I phoned him before I left home and asked him to meet me.

"What's wrong? What's going on?"

I didn't have the heart to tell him and suggested we wait for the doctor. When Kathryn's pediatrician walked in, I fell to pieces.

"Kathryn has a lump under her left nipple," I cried.

Rick looked shocked but not the doctor.

"Let's have a look. Show me exactly what you felt," he said.

I pointed out the lump and then grabbed Rick's hand for support.

"Is it breast cancer?" I asked.

"No, it's her breast."

"Her breast? But she doesn't have one on the other side."

"She will. Just give her some time."

Kathryn was two-months–old when we returned home one afternoon and found a package on our front porch. Inside was a gift wrapped in pink paper and tied with a white satin ribbon. Scrawled across a small card were the words *Love, Daddy*. I remembered mentioning my due date during my father's visit, but I was surprised he remembered.

I ripped off the paper and found a beautiful pink dress and blanket. I stared at the card again. It was the first time in my adult life my father had communicated with me directly. Was it possible he harbored feelings for me? If so, why did he conceal them? I had always assumed he was a heartless person, but maybe he was just a troubled man unable to express love. I wanted to think he cared, but I refused to let my thoughts go there. If he had feelings for me, or for his grandchild, it showed he was human, but that was all it showed. To expect more was to set myself up for disappointment.

I went to my desk and wrote a note thanking him for his gift. Before sealing the envelope, I tucked a photo of Kathryn inside. Later that day, I put his card in my box of keepsakes.

Within months, Kathryn was crawling, and I could barely keep up. Being a full-time mother was exhausting. Forget creative activities designed to stimulate her cognitive development or improve her fine motor skills. I couldn't even maintain a daily schedule.

She absorbed knowledge as a sponge absorbs water and tired of any game or toy within minutes. The only thing I had going for me was the kitchen pantry. For some reason, she never tired of playing among the family staples. I often used this obsession to gain a few hours of personal time. *Personal time,* as any mother with a child under the age of two will tell you, means time to plan a meal, catch up on the laundry or take a bath.

I sat Kathryn on the kitchen floor one morning and surrounded her with a vast array of empty jars and lids. I hoped she would amuse herself long enough for me to do some ironing. I watched her pick a tiny jar and then select a large lid. After numerous attempts to force them together, she dropped them both and crawled away. She sat for a few moments, observing them from a distance, then crawled back and repeated the same process. After more failures, she threw both the jar and lid across the room, lay down and cried. When she finished crying, she looked across the room and crawled toward them again.

I ended her frustration by collecting all the items on the floor and replacing them with her stuffed animals, but her obsession with the jar and lid taught me an important lesson. It reminded me that not all problems can be solved by trying harder or longer. Sometimes, the only answer is to let go and move on.

The phone rang late one night and startled me so badly I dropped the book I was reading. Kathryn had been asleep for hours, so I rushed to catch the call before the phone rang again. I expected to hear Rick's voice since he was out of town, but instead I heard Linda crying.

"Try to calm down. I can't understand what you're saying."

She was silent for a moment and then whispered, "Daddy is dead."

For some reason, I found it impossible to believe.

"How do you know?"

"One of his sisters phoned. Daddy asked her to call me if anything ever happened to him."

There was unmistakable sadness in Linda's voice. During all the years our father had been away, she alone had stayed in touch with him. Although their communication was sporadic, it seemed to help ease some of the pain from her childhood.

While I listened to the details of my father's death, a memory flashed through my mind. Several months ago, Linda had taken her son and daughter to visit our father. They met in St. Louis and went to the zoo. Soon afterward, she stopped by my house to show me pictures from her trip. I glanced through them quickly and handed them back to her.

"You hardly looked at them," she said.

"I'm sorry, but I don't like looking at pictures of our father."

"You should try to forgive Daddy. He regrets the past, but he can't change it."

"He *should* regret it. I hope he regrets it for the rest of his life."

"Here," Linda said, handing me a plastic bag. "It's for Kathryn. Daddy bought it at the zoo and asked me to give it to her."

I looked inside and saw a small white teddy bear with a red bow tied around its neck. After Linda left, I took it to Kathryn's room and placed it on a shelf. I didn't mention where it came from. Why should I? My father was no more a grandfather to her than he was a father to me.

Linda and I spoke for several more minutes before hanging up. She would call Johnny in the morning and then go to our mother's house to give her the news in person.

After our call ended, I sat for a long time thinking about my father. He had never been more than a shadow figure in my life, and yet his imprint was everywhere. The scars left behind by his actions were his only legacy to me.

I put my book down and went to Kathryn's room. I was standing by her bed watching her sleep when my eyes wandered to her bookcase. The white bear was sitting where I had left it. I picked it up and carried it to my room. It was just a small toy. It couldn't have cost much, and it didn't matter to anyone — except to me. It should have been mine, not hers. My father had never given me anything I could hold in my hand and know he had chosen it just for me. I was sitting on my bed, staring at the bear, when a voice flooded my memory and ripped my heart wide open.

"You look so much like your daddy. He misses you, and if he sees you, he might come home."

I sank to the floor, still holding the bear in my hands. My body curled into a tight ball and began to shake. Tears ran down my face, and moans I had never heard before came from somewhere deep inside. I was convinced I had no feelings for my father. Yet, as I lay on the floor crying, the words I heard myself repeating weren't the words of someone who didn't care, nor were they the words of a thirty-year-old woman. They were the words of a four-year-old child still suffering and wanting to know why she wasn't good enough.

"Why didn't you give *me* a bear?" I cried.

I was speaking to an empty room. No one was listening. No one would hear my cries or guess my anguish. It had always been that way. I was a master at hiding my feelings.

I grieved that night for what might have been – for a father who took me to school, pushed me in a swing, ate dinner when I did and tucked me in bed at night. I cried until all the pain was gone, and the regrets were washed away. The past would no longer cripple me. Instead, it would be my guide. The lessons I learned would help me surround my daughter with the love and confidence she deserved. I buried the past and stepped into the future. At least, that's what I thought.

HER STORY, HIS AND MINE 14

There was no reason to think of my father again, and yet I did. He held the key to so many mysteries in my past, and now he was gone. The day we met at Linda's, I let anger and resentment prevent me from seeking answers. Without realizing it, I had squandered the only opportunity I would ever have to hear his story.

My mother was the only person left who knew the truth, but her silence had always communicated the clear message that the subject of my father was off limits. I respected her boundaries as a child, but I no longer was one. I deserved access to a story that was as much mine as it was hers. Gathering my courage, I picked up the phone and dialed her number.

"Mom, I need to talk to you about Daddy. Can I come see you?"

"Do you mean right now? It's after eight o'clock."

"It's important."

I heard a loud sigh and hesitated. She was old, and I was about to reopen wounds that held sorrows she had kept secret for years.

"Can't it at least wait until morning?"

I closed my eyes. I had already waited twenty-two years. That was long enough.

"I'm sorry, but it can't. I'll be there in an hour."

My mother was in her favorite pink robe and slippers when she met me at the door. She called them her comfort clothes, and lately I noticed she kept them on longer in the morning and dressed in them earlier at night. I hated these subtle signs of aging.

She must have sensed my determination because she sat down in her old crushed-velvet Queen Anne chair and prepared herself for my questioning. She looked so fragile. Was I demanding too much? Was I forcing her to revisit moments no one should have to experience twice? I wanted to stop, but I had nowhere else to go, no one else to turn to with my questions.

I sat down on the floor and lay my head on her lap the way I had as a child. She stroked my hair as she spoke, her eyes drifting around the room and then far away into the past.

"Why did he leave? What tore him away from our family?"

"I married a good man. He was kind, generous and thoughtful, but around the time John was born, he changed. He began staying out late at night, and when I asked him where he'd been or whom he'd been with, his answers were vague. He talked about starting a new life in Kansas City. He said he was tired of living in a small Southern town and wanted to move back to the Midwest to be closer to his family.

I was afraid of leaving home. I had three small children, and my marriage was in trouble. I did what most women of my generation did – held my breath and hoped things would improve."

"So when you refused to move, he left without us?"

"He planned a trip to Kansas City to visit his brothers. He said it would be a short trip, too short to take all of us with him. That Saturday, we ate breakfast together, and then he packed a small bag. It was early, and all of you were asleep, but he kissed each of you goodbye before leaving the house. I thought he was experiencing the sort of mid-life crisis that affects many men his age and hoped the trip might do him good.

We were saying good-bye when he handed me an envelope full of cash. I looked inside and found over five hundred dollars. That was a lot of money in those days. When I questioned him about it, he said he'd made a bank deposit the previous day, but it might take several days to clear our account. He wanted to make sure I had enough money in case anything came up while he was away.

After he left, I walked back to the kitchen to finish my coffee, but I couldn't stop thinking about the money. Something about it seemed peculiar. I went to our bedroom and discovered that nearly half of his clothes were missing. That was when I realized he wasn't coming back. Even if he had wanted to return, it wouldn't have been possible."

"Why?"

She didn't speak, and her frail hand covered her eyes while her lips trembled.

"Mom, are you all right?"

There was no response, so I ran to the kitchen for some water and tissues. I hadn't seen my mother cry in a long time. She was a strong woman not given to displays of emotion.

"He left because he was involved with another woman," she said quietly.

It was all she could do to say the words, and I wondered how many times she had ever done so. I put my arm around her shoulders and tried to calm her. I had forced her to disclose events she probably thought she would never have to think of again. She didn't deserve this – none of us did.

When she spoke again, her voice sounded less anxious, and I wondered if sharing her secret was helping to lessen the pain.

"The woman was well-known in our community. She was also married and had children. She was attending a church revival one night when her conscience directed her to renounce her sins with your father – in front of the entire congregation. When news of their affair became public, it was ugly. My parents never got over it. It broke my father's heart."

Another woman? My father left because of another woman? Bit by bit, so many things began to make sense. The trip to Kansas, the secrets and the silence. Growing up, there were times when I felt like secrecy was another member of our family. Because no one ever mentioned my father, I suspected it had something to do with him, and I was right.

I thought my mother was finished, but she continued.

"The Monday after your father left, I went to the bank and learned that, except for a few thousand dollars, he'd emptied all our joint accounts. Even with my job, I'm not sure what we would have done without the rental properties your grandfather left us."

My father's character was growing darker by the minute. Not only was he an unscrupulous, two-timing son-of-a-bitch, he was also a thief who stole food from the mouths of his own children. This was the same person who, less than six years ago, drove through town and had the audacity to call and see if he could stop by and say hello. If I had known then what I knew now, I would have met him at the front door with a much different greeting.

"When Daddy left, what explanation did you give us? Even if Johnny or I didn't have questions, Linda was six and must have asked about him."

"None of you were old enough to understand what was happening. Things were different then. Divorce was rare and never discussed openly. Linda wouldn't have known what it meant, much less you or John.

I said your father was in Kansas City visiting his family because you had been there and knew it was far away. I hoped it would give you some-thing to hold onto during your first months without him."

"It couldn't have taken Linda long to realize he wasn't coming back. What did you tell her?"

My mother sighed and let her body relax into the folds of her chair. I should have stopped my interrogating and insisted she go to bed, but I couldn't. It had taken me twenty-two years to hear this story, and I was too selfish to give up the only opportunity I might ever have of knowing the truth.

"From the moment Linda was born, she and your father were inseparable. She worshiped him, but he left without even telling her good-bye. I tried to explain he would be gone a long time, but she wouldn't listen. She would push me away and go stand at the door and watch for him. I was getting dressed for work one morning when she came to my room and asked why he left. I think you and John must have heard what she said because I looked up and you were both standing in the doorway.

I said Daddy went away because he stopped loving us. He wasn't happy with us anymore."

I bolted upright and stared into my mother's face. I was speechless. Didn't she understand the gravity of her statement? She had linked us to her failed marriage. Why had she laid such an awful burden on us? Perhaps what she told us seemed genuine to her at the time, but it was even more devastating than the truth. No child should have to hear such heart-breaking words.

"You took me to see Daddy once. We went alone, but I can't recall where it was or why we were there."

My mother looked startled.

"You were so young. I didn't know you remembered. A few months after we separated, your father phoned to let me know he would be in town on business the following week. He asked if I wanted to see him. I said I did, and we agreed to meet at his hotel. I took you with me, but it was a mistake. I thought when he saw you he might have a change of heart, but he didn't, and it upset you terribly."

'*Upset me terribly?*' My mother exploited my innocence, and for years, I suffered from low self-esteem. As a child, I cast myself as a failure – the one unable to save her family. In actuality, I had probably done more than could be expected of any small child whose family was in the midst of such an immense crisis.

It would take time to process everything my mother shared, but I finally had my story. It wasn't pretty, and there was plenty of blame to go around, but at least it was honest and whole.

I wondered how much needless anxiety, mistakes and pain could have been avoided if the truth had been shared earlier. Perhaps none . . . maybe all.

My mother looked relieved when I told her I was finished with my questions. I helped her to bed and then, in spite of the cold weather, went outside for some fresh air. As soon as I looked up, a star shot across the sky. I made a wish and sat down on the top step of the porch – the same step I was standing on the first time I told Rick I loved him.

Now that I knew my story, it wasn't difficult to understand why I found it so hard to trust others with my feelings or why I expected every-one to walk away. At a critical point in my life, someone *had* walked away; someone I loved and trusted. I thought the relationships I ran through dur-ing my adolescence were a search for love, but I was wrong. I was searching for someone to replace my father.

A cold wind caught my attention, and I noticed dew was beginning to accumulate on the grass. It was late and time to be in bed. The details shared with me were distressing, but I knew I would sleep well that night. After all these years, my conscience was finally clear.

MY MOTLEY CREW 15

I kissed my daughter goodbye and relinquished responsibility for her well-being to a woman I had known for less than an hour. As I walked away, I felt Kathryn's eyes on me.

"Don't be late," she called.

I turned and took a mental snapshot of her standing in the doorway of her classroom. She had one foot planted in the room and the other in the hallway where I stood. Her body language suggested she was prepared to stay but would be just as happy to leave.

She chose her favorite outfit to wear — a turquoise Oshkosh B'gosh jumper. Inside her red backpack were new crayons, a couple of fat pencils, an Elmer's Glue Stick and a pair of blunt scissors. Crayons, pencils, glue and scissors aren't much to give a little person about to face the world on her own, but I wasn't worried. Confidence, determination and cheerfulness were also at her disposal and mattered far more than what her bag held.

For the past five years, my life had centered on preparing her for this day. Every letter and number she learned, every trip to the park we made, every scheduled play date and song we sang - all of it had been carefully orchestrated to move her one step closer to independence. Yet as I watched her standing on the threshold of Mrs. Vaden's kindergarten classroom, what I wanted most at that moment was for her to throw her arms around my legs and beg me not to leave. It wasn't fair - this whole *letting go* business.

I suddenly remembered the day Kathryn sat on the kitchen floor struggling to make a large lid fit on top of a small jar. I had almost forgotten what she taught me that day – *Sometimes the only answer is to let go and move on.* That's what I would have to learn to do.

When the time came to choose a school for Kathryn, we opted out of a prep school that hailed its test scores as if they were worthy of a Nobel Prize and instead chose a school with a philosophy compatible with our own. It emphasized that learning to navigate life was just as essential as learning to accelerate through it, and learning to live well together was of equal value to learning to compete. We never regretted our decision.

Like most parents, we did our best to encourage our child's interests, but success was always hit or miss. The previous day, I observed Kathryn's ballet class.

"All together now. Right foot tap, left foot tap, knees apart and left foot tap . . ."

It was a humbling experience. Kathryn did her best to follow her teacher's instructions, but in spite of the pink ribbon on her right shoe and the blue one on her left, it was obvious she couldn't tell her feet apart. It was time to end this torturous, weekly experience and face reality: Kathryn would never dance the role of Clara in *The Nutcracker*. She might not even reach snowflake or sugarplum status.

Ballet was one more activity to cross off our list. First came swimming; the memory of her floating face up under the water still gave me nightmares. Then there was gymnastics. There are only so many times a parent can watch her child bounce off a trampoline and hit the ground before calling it quits. Her endeavors in the theater? They weren't worth the language she picked up behind stage. We knew one day she would discover her niche, and it would be soon . . . maybe.

The year Kathryn entered kindergarten; I pursued a Master's Degree in Special Education. Thanks to my trustworthy babysitter next door and a husband who did the laundry and kept Domino's Pizza on speed dial, I completed my degree in four semesters. Shortly afterward, I joined the Special Education Department of an elementary school in rural Middle Tennessee. Actually, since there was only enough money to fund one position that year, I *was* the Special Education Department.

I approached my work with the undeserved confidence new degrees impart. Why shouldn't I? I knew every technique and method known to help learning disabled students. Sadly, I soon learned the children occupying the desks in my classroom were in need of far more than my technical expertise. They were socially immature, emotionally stunted and academically challenged. The question was whether I could make a difference.

The students assigned to me were shared property. They spent an average of three hours a day in my classroom working on basic skills in reading, writing and mathematics, but the majority of their time was in a regular classroom. The transition wasn't always easy. Sitting in a regular classroom meant they had to compete with students who neither carried the stigma nor faced the difficulties associated with being learning disabled.

I found most teachers willing to make whatever accommodations were necessary to insure their special needs students met with some measure of success. However, a few were firm in their conviction that *any* student placed in their classroom, for whatever amount of time, should be required to do the same work at the same pace as all other students. This insensitive and unreasonable expectation not only deprived my special needs students of their right to appropriate accommodations but also left them vulnerable to formidable attacks by their peers. I watched their confidence plummet and self-esteem evaporate. These callous, inflexible teachers inspired me to create *the safe room*.

The safe room was nothing more than a large storage closet in my classroom - a room within a room. Nevertheless, it was private, accessible and soundproof – the latter attribute being its most essential. When confronted with the inevitable frustration and humiliation brought on by being unable to compete with their peers, my students could excuse themselves from their regular classroom and go in the safe room to vent their anger.

Word spreads quickly in a small school, and before long, the safe room was a popular place. Children I didn't even know began lining up to use it. I felt like the host at a popular restaurant.

"I'm sorry but the safe room is full at the moment. If you care to leave your name, I can contact you when space becomes available."

Things quickly got out of control, and I asked my students for a solution. After careful consideration and much debate, they decided they had first, but not exclusive, right to the safe room. I thought their decision was just. After all, they were the ones who cleaned out the closet in the first place.

My students were a motley but tenderhearted crew. Seated on my right was Chris, a nervous, excitable boy of ten who gnawed his fingernails so short they sometimes bled. When both his parents took two jobs, his fifteen-year-old brother became his guardian. That arrangement ended when his brother went to prison for possession of drugs – a fact made known to the county sheriff by his brother's disgruntled pregnant girlfriend, also fifteen.

Jesse sat next to Chris. He was a strapping farm boy who rarely bathed or changed clothes. He came to school each day wearing the same shoes he wore when he fed his pigs. I kept a bar of soap and a towel in my desk for Jesse. He only used them if he absolutely had to – meaning that three times before noon, someone looked around and asked, "Does anyone else smell shit?"

Nine-year-old Jacob sat across the aisle from Jesse. His mother and father owned an auto repair shop. Everywhere Jesse had dirt; Jacob had grease. In spite of his five years of school, he could barely read. What he *could* do was take a car engine apart and put it back together. I know because I saw him do it. Despite his numerous academic limitations, he was one of the happiest children I ever met.

I wish I could say the same for Davis. He joined us a few months after school started. His record showed he had attended three different schools the prior year. He worked hard but made little progress, and his lack of social interaction worried me. He never made a sound and only spoke when asked a question. The most I ever got from him was a "yes, ma'am" or "no, ma'am." I knew something was wrong and worried about him more than all my other boys.

Davis arrived at school one morning earlier than usual. I didn't see him come in or hang up his coat. Like always, he was in his seat before anyone knew he was there. A short time later, I looked up and found Jesse standing in my doorway.

"I think you better check on Davis. He don't look so good."

Something in Jessie's eyes alarmed me and I followed him out of my office. Davis was sitting at his desk with his head buried in his arms. I went over and knelt beside him. When I put my hand on his back, his entire body shuddered.

"Davis," I whispered, "come with me. I need to talk to you."

He stood and turned toward me. I covered my mouth but not before an audible gasp escaped. His face looked like it had been used as a punching bag. His eyes were swollen shut and his upper lip was twice its normal size. His bruises had already turned a horrible shade of blue, and I knew they would get worse. He was almost unrecognizable, and I feared that beneath his clothes other parts of his body might be in similar condition. After sending Chris for the principal, I laid my hand gently on his back and directed him to my office.

"Can you tell me what happened? Who did this to you?"

"My dad."

"Do you know why he did it?"

"I got mad at my dog last night and kicked him. Dad told me never to do it again. He said he'd show me what it felt like so I wouldn't forget."

I wasn't unfamiliar with the plight of abused or neglected children. As a teacher, I had bandaged up wounds, washed faces, fed, clothed and testified in court on behalf of my students. However, nothing ever sickened me more than the battered face of that quiet, mild-mannered little boy.

A caseworker from the Department of Human Services arrived to take Davis for a medical exam and treatment. Before they left, I asked where he go afterwards.

"He'll be placed in an emergency foster home until a determination is made about his future."

His future? What hope was there for his future? I said goodbye to Davis and went back to my classroom.

"Is Davis gonna be all right?" asked Jesse.

"I hope so. He's in pretty bad shape."

"I bet his father done it," Jacob said.

"Why do you think so? Did Davis tell you something?"

"No, ma'am, but I seen his father, and he's mean. One time I saw him slap Davis."

"When was that?"

"It was one day when Davis and him come to the shop. Davis was drinking a soda, but he dropped it when he tried to get in the car."

"Did it spill on something? Is that why his father was angry?"

"No, ma'am. It just spilled on the floor. His dad was mad 'cause Davis wasted that soda. He said sodas cost too much to waste, and then he slapped Davis real hard."

I dismissed the children and went to my office. How could I help Davis? He was a powerless child, a victim of an abusive father. Research shows that most abusive parents were abused children. How does that cycle end? Is there any hope for Davis or children like him?

I reached across my desk to turn on the lamp but stopped when tears began streaming down my face. I didn't want light. The darkness might help erase the image of Davis from my mind or the downcast faces of my students – children trying to understand something even I couldn't grasp.

My normally full school bag was almost empty when I left for home that day. I didn't intend to work that night. All I planned to do was hold my daughter and tell her how much she was worth.

CREATING PHOBIAS 16

During the years that followed, I vacillated between an urge to accelerate through life and a desire to apply the brakes. The status quo was a myth. What existed one day evolved into something else the next. Our lives were in a constant state of flux, and the middle ground shifted daily. In other words, we had a teenager in the family.

The same week I finished my Master's Degree, Rick began working on an MBA at Vanderbilt. He was in the second year of his program when he turned forty. With the help of his study partners, I kidnapped him that evening and checked us into an expensive hotel. We feasted on a gourmet dinner at a romantic restaurant overlooking the city, took the elevator to our beautiful room with a king size bed and fell asleep. The story of our lives during those years involved lots of work and very little play.

On the morning of *my* fortieth birthday, I stood in front of the mirror, looked myself in the eye and announced I would never be young again. Contrary to the claims of cosmetic companies everywhere, time was no longer on my side. Still, I refused to give in without a fight – a fight that ultimately proved more hazardous than turning forty.

First, I started jogging. Regardless of the weather, I hit the road every day and didn't stop until I finished a five-mile run. Next, I cut down on calories, way down, and returned to my pre-college weight. My wardrobe morphed into a stylish collection of youthful attire, and new highlights gave my hair a natural glow. Somehow, I had managed to turn back the hands of time . . . or so I thought until I woke up one morning with a pain in my back so excruciating it forced me to my knees. An hour later, I was in the emergency room.

"All I did was get out of bed," I told the doctor. "That's all. I just got out of bed."

The doctor's verdict was a herniated disc. He told me to lie flat on my back for two weeks or I would end up in surgery. I followed the doctor's orders and within two weeks gained seven pounds. I no longer fit into my fashionable clothes and moved like someone twice my age.

Fortunately, juggling the roles of wife, mother and teacher didn't allow me much time to grieve over the loss of my once eye-catching appearance. My days began at five o'clock. when I showered, dressed for work, packed lunches, cooked breakfast and checked Kathryn's choice of school attire. I then dashed out the door to teach the first of seven classes that started at seven thirty. and ended at three o'clock The second I left work, I jumped in the car and drove insanely fast to Kathryn's school, picked her up and deposited her at either tennis matches or piano lessons. Piano, by the way, was the niche we tried to help Kathryn discover. The moment she sat at a piano, it was obvious to everyone that it was both her talent and her love. Life was busy, but it was never without music.

When I reached home each afternoon, it was time to return phone calls, do laundry, cook dinner, supervise homework and get Kathryn off to bed. For the most part, those years went smoothly. Still, like all families, we had times when our good intentions backfired . . .

"We're going out for dinner? Doesn't Kathryn have school tomorrow?" Rick asked over the phone.

"Yes, but the book I'm reading says it's best to confront your teenager in neutral territory – a place where she can't just walk away."

"Kathryn never walks away when we're speaking to her."

"Not yet, but there's always a first."

"I think you're taking this book too seriously."

"That's a fine thing to say. You should appreciate the effort I'm making to help guide our daughter through the most difficult years of her life. Don't you realize how easy it is to be influenced by the wrong person and end up making bad decisions that lead to poor self-esteem?"

"You're right. Make the reservation."

"What changed your mind?"

"I had a flashback."

I didn't have to ask of who. I hung up and immediately booked a table for three.

The incident generating the need for this emergency family meeting was accidental, or at least that would be my story when asked how I happened to be in possession of the note hidden in my purse. In truth, I found it while trying to organize Kathryn's school materials. In other words, I cleaned out her backpack and took the liberty of examining its contents. In the process, I came across a letter written by one of her friends. Its sexual overtones and objectionable language needed addressing – and they would be – in the neutral territory of her favorite restaurant later that night.

Rick was already seated when we arrived. It was rare for us to go out on a school night and Kathryn was in high spirits. I waited until she finished her order of spinach/artichoke dip before making my move.

"So, how is school going?" I asked.

"Okay," she replied.

"How are your friends?"

"Okay."

"And Suzanne? How is she doing?"

"Fine."

"Do you see much of her at school?"

"Sometimes."

"When you see her, is she acting appropriately?"

"Mom, why are you asking all these questions?"

"I happened to see this note yesterday and it concerns me."

I retrieved the letter from my purse and laid it beside her dinner plate. An expression of horror fell across her face.

"You went through my backpack?"

"Is that where you found this?" Rick asked. "You went through her bag?"

The tables had turned, and suddenly *I* was under scrutiny.

"I *wasn't* going through your bag. I was just helping organize it."

"I can't believe you went through my things. I thought you trusted me."

Kathryn was on the verge of tears, and Rick didn't look too happy either.

"She does have a right to her personal space," Rick said.

If looks could kill, Rick would no longer be with us. I glared at him and wanted to scream, "Whose side are you on?"

"Kathryn, you know Mom and I trust you. Mom is just concerned about the kind of influence Suzanne might have on you. When you surround yourself with people who don't have the same values you have, it's easy to find yourself pressured into making wrong choices. Neither of us wants to see you hurt."

"You don't have to worry, Dad. I think Suzanne makes up stuff just to get attention. I would never let myself be pressured into doing something I knew was wrong."

"That's good. I know we can trust you and you can trust us never to go through your things again."

Kathryn looked at Rick with love and admiration and then looked at me with disappointment and indignation. I looked at her with a smidgen of skepticism but decided to drop the whole matter. Even so, it was several years before I could suggest going out to dinner without her turning pale and asking why.

Over time, it became clear that embedded in my decision-making was the subconscious fear Kathryn would make the same mistakes I did. I scrutinized her actions and motives through the lens of my own experiences, not hers. My commitment to helping her maneuver her teenage years successfully was sincere and unwavering, but my parenting skills suffered from inexperience. If asked to write a book about my unique approach, the title would have been something like, *Parenting by Trial and Error: The Art of Confusing Your Child and Creating Phobias*. I often prayed love would make up for what I lacked in wisdom.

CROSSING THE DELAWARE 17

The University of Pennsylvania came knocking on our door one day with an offer destined to test our boundaries, force our hand and change our lives forever. Worst of all, it threatened to unravel what Rick and I cherished most — our marriage.

The University of Pennsylvania was the least recognized member of the eight private universities comprising the Ivy League, and its innovative programs and illustrious history were unknown to many. However, that was about to change. There are rare moments in history when events align themselves in perfect order and amazing things are accomplished. In 1996, Penn benefitted from just such a moment.

The Trustees of the University of Pennsylvania included some of the most brilliant minds of our generation, and their collective wealth wasn't too shabby either. As important as their net worth and intellects were, however, their most important contribution to Penn was their dedication. The Trustees' strategic plan included some of the boldest and most creative initiatives ever attempted by a university. If they succeeded in their mission, not only would Penn's future be secure but also the future of West Philadelphia.

The trustees were not alone in their resolve. Penn's new president, Dr. Judith Rodin, herself an alumna of Penn, was passionate about the institution and worked diligently on its behalf. Between the Trustees' resources, which were effectively limitless, and Rodin's dedication, a new prominence for Penn was all but guaranteed.

At age thirty-four, Penn's new Executive Vice-President, John Fry, was young but not inexperienced. He understood that the success of the Trustees' strategic plan depended on strengthening Penn's infrastructure, and his first priority was to build a management team of accomplished administrators.

The audit departments within Penn and its health system were in dire need of restructuring – preferably by someone with experience in overseeing both entities. Rick had the expertise John needed, and he was determined to bring Rick to Penn. Rick had accomplished everything he hoped to achieve at Vanderbilt and yearned for new challenges. Penn's aggressive agenda intrigued him, but after struggling with his decision, he initially declined John's offer. Although the opportunity was substantial, so were the risks. He was still agonizing over his decision when a second, even more generous, offer arrived. He asked me to reconsider my position, and I agreed with great apprehension. I needed solace, so I turned to the stars.

When I was a child, my mother taught me to recognize star patterns. It was fascinating to look up and find the same stars in their familiar places each night. I looked up now and searched for the Big Dipper.

"Nancy, did you hear anything I just said?"

I ignored Rick's question and focused on the sky. It was a pointless, immature tactic, but I wanted to postpone our confrontation for as long as possible.

"Nancy?"

"You said I don't have to make up my mind tonight, but you have to give Penn an answer by next week. I'm obstinate, not deaf."

Rick shook his head. It was an unconscious action on his part, but it never failed to irk me. What right did he have to be irritated? I deserved more patience than I was getting.

"Why are you determined to pursue this? You have a great job, and we like Nashville.

Have you thought of what this might do to our marriage or what it would mean for Kathryn?"

"I've thought of nothing else for days. I know it will require a lot from all of us, but this is an extraordinary opportunity. I know we can make it work.

I can fly to Philadelphia on Monday mornings and fly home on Friday nights. You and Kathryn can stay in Nashville until she finishes high school, and then we would relocate to Philadelphia. It's a unique city, and I think you'd enjoy living there."

He took my hands and held them in his.

"Penn is poised to push every boundary in higher education, and I'd like to be a part of that change. We've discussed all of this a hundred times, but if you want me to tell Penn the answer is no, then I will."

"I've never even been to Philadelphia," I said.

"You have only yourself to blame. You were given numerous opportunities to visit, but you refused every offer."

"I didn't think you were serious enough to warrant a visit. Besides, Kathryn won't graduate for another two years. Anything could happen in two years. You might decide you don't like working at Penn or you don't want to live in Philadelphia."

"If I go, I intend to stay."

Rick's response shook me. He had always been the giving one, the selfless one. If I expected more from him than I did from myself, it was because he had always *been more*. I felt like crying, but instead I lashed back.

"Just go. Leave. I don't care."

I left him and went inside to get ready for bed. We had been best friends for over twenty years and rarely argued. It wasn't that we were uniquely compatible, because we weren't. When we met, we were complete opposites, and in spite of how much our taste had changed over the years, we still were. The harmony in our marriage was due solely to Rick. He had loved me through every stage of my life and given me the security I needed to reach for my dreams.

I turned off the light and tried to sleep. I didn't hear him come in, but it wasn't long before I felt his arm around me and his head resting against my shoulder.

"I didn't mean for this to become so complicated. Maybe we should just forget the whole thing," he said.

I rolled over and faced him. I couldn't help running my fingers through his hair. It was thick and wavy. I thought it was beautiful, but he referred to it as a curse and spent hours trying to straighten it.

"I didn't mean what I said. You know I care. I don't want to stand in your way if this is something you really want to do."

"It's late. We'll talk about it tomorrow."

Talk about it tomorrow? That was the last thing I wanted to hear before falling asleep.

I woke up during the night and went back outside to think. I knew delaying this decision would only make matters worse, but I didn't have an answer – at least not one that seemed fair. Rick had never asked anything of me, so how could I say no? I wanted to share his excitement, but disturbing thoughts kept entering my mind and refused to be silenced. *He wants to leave. If he cared, he wouldn't go. If I were enough, he would stay.* Old feelings of insecurity resurfaced and fed off my fear of rejection. Nevertheless, the following morning I told him my answer was yes. With my support secured, he prepared to resign his position.

Although his resignation caught Vanderbilt Chancellor Joe Wyatt by surprise, he offered Rick his full support. After their meeting, Rick raced back to his office and phoned to tell me it was official. In one month, he would leave Vanderbilt to work for the University of Pennsylvania. In two years, Philadelphia would become our new home. I told myself not to worry; a lot could happen in two years.

Kathryn's winter break gave us the opportunity to make our first family trip to Philly. On the morning of our inaugural journey, we arrived at the airport eager to begin our two-hour flight. If we had been aware of the Philadelphia International Airport's reputation for delayed flights, we would have showed up later and with less enthusiasm.

It was after six o'clock and already dark by the time we reached Philly. Unlike Nashville, the City of Brotherly Love was experiencing the bitter sting of winter. We exited the airport and scurried to find a cab.

On the ride into Center City, I noticed patches of ice floating on the Schuylkill River and thought of Emanuel Leutze's painting of *Washington Crossing the Delaware*. The painting depicts General Washington and his brave soldiers maneuvering the treacherous ice-filled waters of the Delaware River. We were making our own crossing that day and perhaps one as daring as Washington's. In 1996, the crime-filled streets of Philadelphia no doubt held as many perils as navigating the icy waters of the Delaware.

When we arrived in West Philadelphia, we were unable to locate Rick's new apartment. After circling the block three times, our cabbie called it quits. Between his Middle Eastern accent and Rick's southern drawl, communication broke down.

"Just let us off at the next corner," Rick grumbled.

We exited the cab and continued our search on foot. A brutal gust of wind whipped around the corner of 36th Street and caught me by surprise.

I clutched the collar of my coat and trudged ahead. The thin jacket I chose for the trip epitomized how ill prepared I was for my new surroundings. Nothing about me seemed right, not my clothes, my accent or my vocabulary. I felt like I had stumbled into a private club where it was obvious to everyone, including myself, that I didn't belong.

"Rick, are you sure we're walking in the right direction? I'm freezing."

"It won't be much longer. Lancaster Avenue is at the top of this hill. We'll be there in less than five minutes."

We reached the corner and found the old red brick building housing the apartment that would be Rick's home-away-from-home for the next two years. It was only three blocks from campus, but I doubted it was safe to walk through the neighborhood after dark.

We made our way to the front door of the apartment house, and I noticed flowers on each side of the front entrance that lay blackened and abandoned in the cold. Their pots now served the more practical function of collecting cigarettes. The awning overhead was torn and flapped violently in the wind. Barely distinguishable across its front were the words *Old Quaker*. We looked at each other, but no one spoke. It was hard to imagine anything quaint or charming awaiting us behind the doors.

Rick reached into his pocket for an envelope that held the keys and codes we needed to gain entry into the building. Additional keys to a rental car would be in his apartment. We stepped into a narrow foyer and took the elevator to the second floor.

My first impression of the apartment wasn't bad. I was surprised to discover soaring fourteen-foot ceilings with beautiful wood beams and seven-foot windows that made the small apartment feel larger than it actually was. Unfortunately, we soon felt a distinct northern breeze coming through those windows, and what little warm air existed rose to the top of the fourteen-foot ceilings. Someone had apparently decided impressive architectural features trumped basic human needs such as warmth.

Kathryn explored the apartment while Rick and I made a list of groceries. It wasn't until after we finished our list that we realized we had no idea where to find a market.

"I noticed a Seven Eleven a few blocks away," Rick said. "I'll go pick up some food while the two of you make a list of things we need for the apartment."

Rick buttoned his coat and pulled on his gloves. Before he left, I kissed him goodbye. After noting all the abandoned buildings and makeshift shelters along Lancaster Avenue, I wasn't convinced I would ever see him again.

After Rick left, I handed Kathryn some paper and asked her to prioritize a list of things we needed for the apartment. A few minutes later, I saw TV, VCR, phone, stereo and computer scribbled across the page. I hastily added blankets.

Rick soon returned and emptied the contents of his bag on the kitchen table. He had brought a loaf of bread, a jar of peanut butter, a gallon of milk, some coffee and a bag of Skittles.

"That's it? That's all they had?"

"No, they also carry cigarettes and beer."

I knew the sarcasm in his voice was due to a long and stressful day, so I let it pass. We ate peanut butter sandwiches, drank our milk, popped a handful of Skittles into our mouths and headed for a department store . . . if we could find one.

We drove around aimlessly for over an hour before I convinced Rick to stop and ask for directions. When he did, we learned there was a Sears store not far away, which should have everything we needed. It did, and two hours later, we loaded our bounty into the trunk of our rental car and headed back to the Old Quaker.

After hauling everything inside, we collapsed on the sofa. We had been in Philadelphia for less than five hours and were already exhausted, hungry and broke.

"I don't know about the two of you, but I'm ready for bed," I said.

"Mom, where am I going to sleep?"

We had been in such a rush when we arrived that I hadn't taken time to look around the apartment. Until that moment, I didn't realize we only had one bed. Convincing Kathryn to sleep on the living room couch wouldn't be easy, but I had to try.

"You can sleep on the couch. It's huge, and you'll have the TV all to yourself," I said.

"Please don't make me sleep out here alone! If someone broke in, I would be the first one found. I'd be dead before I could even scream for help!"

"Calm down," Rick snapped. "No one is getting murdered here tonight. If it makes you feel better, you can sleep with Mom, and I'll sleep on the couch."

"It might be best for a while," I said.

We were all in bed within minutes. I wrapped a new blanket around me and tried to ignore the cold air penetrating the seven-foot windows I initially thought added so much character to the apartment. I was still cold, so I inched further down under the covers.

"Mom, do you think Dad will be happy here? Won't he be lonely?" Kathryn asked.

"To be honest, I think it's going to be a lot harder than he realizes."

I kissed her goodnight and lay beside her until she fell asleep. Afterward, I crawled out of bed and felt my way to the living room couch.

"Are you asleep?" I whispered.

"No. Crawl in if you can find any room."

I crawled under the blankets and curled up next to him.

"Do you like the apartment?"

"It's okay. I don't expect to spend much time here. It's just a place to sleep."

"It's not just a place to sleep. It's a place to live - a place to start a new life. Don't forget, our next chapter begins here."

He didn't speak, and it was in those quiet moments that I first realized how unhappy he was.

"We both knew a transition as big as this one would require a lot. This is day one of a seven hundred and thirty-day adventure. I have no idea what lies ahead, but whatever it is, I know we'll help each other through it."

"What would I do without you?"

"I'm not sure, but you'll find out in the next seven-hundred and twenty-nine days."

He was asleep within minutes but not me. The streetlights outside lit up the unfamiliar room where we lay and left me feeling disoriented and depressed. I hoped my fringed optimism helped because in truth, all I wanted was to get back on a plane to Nashville and pretend none of this had ever happened. I lay in Rick's arms wishing we were home in our own room and our own bed.

The sound of laughter broke the silence. I inched my way off the couch and peered out the window. Half a dozen men were sitting on the sidewalk below rolling dice in a game of craps. Brown paper bags barely disguised the liquor sitting by their sides.

Just then, a trolley barreled down Lancaster Avenue with its brakes screeching as it turned onto 36th Street. Good Lord, how would we ever get any sleep? That was when it hit me. The craps game, the drunken laughter, the screeching of the trolley and the glare from the outside lights . . . nothing was disturbing the slumber of my family. *I* was the only one still awake.

I stumbled back to the couch, pulled the blanket up to my chin and closed my eyes.

Someone yelled, "Dice be nice!"

Soon afterward, I fell asleep.

SEVEN-HUNDRED AND THIRTY DAYS 18

We spent the next week familiarizing ourselves with Philly and organizing Rick's apartment. I thought personal belongings would make the apartment feel more like home, but as I hung a picture of our family on the wall, I realized a home isn't replicated just by filling space with familiar objects.

A week later, it was time to leave Philly and time to say goodbye to Rick. Before we closed the door of the apartment, I took one last look around. Everything seemed so wrong. Why were Rick's shirts hanging in *that* closet? Why was a picture of our family sitting on the table beside *that* couch? None of those things belonged here. They belonged at home and so did Rick.

It took all the self-control I could muster not to cry when we said goodbye at the airport. Kathryn's tears were enough for all of us. Rick tried hard to conceal his emotions, but his strength couldn't make this easier for us; nothing could.

"I'll see you both in two weeks," he said, as he removed our luggage from the car. "Take care of each other, and don't argue."

Before I disappeared into the airport, I turned and looked at him one last time. He smiled and waved. After all these years, didn't he know I could read his heart?

Hours later, we boarded our plane. Kathryn stretched out in an empty seat beside us and fell asleep. We were close to take off when a flight attendant approached me.

"Is Mr. Whitfield joining you today?"

"What did you say?"

"I asked if Mr. Whitfield will be flying today. His name is on our passenger list, but he hasn't checked in. This empty seat is his."

"Oh. No, I am sorry. He won't be joining us."

It didn't occur to me that the empty seat in our row belonged to Rick. I had forgotten about the round trip ticket we bought to take advantage of a better fare. The attendant's innocent question was like a stab to my heart.

Chinese philosopher, Lao Tzu wrote, "The longest journey begins with a single step." Ours began with a single flight. It was the first of many flights, phone calls, letters and emails that spanned the next two years of my life.

I turned and glanced out the window just as the sun shot one final blast of brilliant color across the sky. A few minutes later, it was dark. I checked to make sure Kathryn was still asleep, then lay my head back and cried.

It was late when I pulled our car in the driveway. Sleet was falling, and the drive from the airport had been treacherous. Kathryn was asleep, and I wasn't looking forward to waking her. Winter break was behind us, and she would have to be up early the next morning for school.

As I turned the car toward the garage, the headlights fell across a letter hanging from the door. I stopped the car, maneuvered across the ice and retrieved it. The note was from the Gas Department.

"This is your third and final notice. If we have not received a response from you by January 3rd, we will have no alternative but to discontinue service."

A knot formed in my stomach. Today was January 4. How could this happen? Rick always paid our bills on time. There had to be a mistake. A string of obscenities was about to cross my lips when a distressing scenario entered my mind. Was it possible Rick had been so busy preparing for his move to Philly that he had forgotten to pay the bills? What kind of man would desert his family in January without paying the gas bill? My longing gave way to anger.

After getting Kathryn settled in her room, I went downstairs to the garage to bring up our luggage. I opened the car trunk, took one look at our bags and decided to unpack the next day. Weary does not begin to describe how I felt.

I climbed back up the stairs to the kitchen and was about to turn off the lights when I noticed the mail. A friend had picked it up while we were away and stacked it in the middle of the kitchen table. Looking at it reminded me of the notice from the Gas Department. I unbuttoned my coat, poured a glass of wine and checked the pile for anything of importance. My eyes quickly landed on a letter from our insurance company. I tore open the envelope and pulled out the letter.

"We regret that unless your premium is paid in full by January 6th, the insurance on your home will expire at midnight on January 7th. This is your third and final notice. Please contact us to resolve this problem and avoid interruption in your coverage."

Wine sloshed over the rim of my glass and landed on the stack of mail in front of me. I grabbed a towel and blotted envelopes. There had to be a mistake. Rick would never allow this to happen.

I soon discovered my faith was unjustified. As I rummaged through the mail, I found two similar bills and four overdraft notices from our bank.

I knew how hectic Rick's schedule was during his last month at home, and I could easily forgive an unpaid bill or two, but I'd offered to help numerous times. Each time he'd assured me everything was under control. The disaster lying on our kitchen table was evidence to the contrary. I was fuming as I reached for the phone and dialed his apartment.

"Hello?"

"Were you asleep?"

"Yes, but it's okay. Is everything all right at home? It's after one o'clock. Did you just get home?"

"No, I've been here awhile."

"Is everything all right?"

"No, something's missing."

"What! What's missing?"

"The heat."

There was a long pause.

"The heat was cut off because the bill wasn't paid. Neither was the bill from our insurance company. They're threatening to cancel our policy. We also have four overdraft notices from the bank."

"I can explain."

"No, I don't think so. Not tonight, and maybe not tomorrow either. I'll call when I'm ready to talk."

I hung up and looked at the pile of mail on the table. I didn't want to think about the heat, bills, or Philadelphia. In a few minutes, I would climb the stairs to an empty bedroom. That was enough to handle for one night.

I got ready for bed and set the alarm, something Rick usually did. In spite of my flannel pajamas, socks and a thick blanket, I had to pull the covers up to my neck to keep warm. It's surprising how much colder a bed can be when there's only one person in it.

Why was it so dark? It was the lack of street lamps, of course. Those stupid lights would never hinder my sleep again. Yet, I wasn't sleeping. It was too quiet. There were no craps games, squealing trolleys or sirens to contend with, but there was also no snoring, no one turning over in bed, no one to put his arm around me in the middle of the night or curl up next to me. My initial bliss suddenly felt like hell more than heaven, and my emotions flip-flopped between longing and despair. I reached for the phone and dialed Rick's apartment.

"Hello?"

"Did I wake you up?"

"Yes, but I don't mind."

"I can't sleep. I hate going to bed alone."

"I know. I hate it, too."

"Not enough to keep you awake."

"I was only half-asleep."

"I don't believe you."

"I don't blame you. If I were you, I wouldn't believe me either. You trusted me, and I let you down."

"It's no more your fault than mine. It was unreasonable to expect you to manage everything at home and in Philadelphia. I'll take responsibility for things here. It will be good for me. I've allowed myself to become dependent on you, and that was a mistake."

"We'll talk about it tomorrow. You should get some sleep. Promise me you won't lie awake worrying about the bills. We'll work everything out tomorrow."

"There's nothing to work out. As of tonight, I'm taking charge of things at home and you're taking charge of things in Philadelphia."

"There's no reason to be rash."

"Rash? We have no heat, no credibility with our bank and we're in danger of losing the insurance on our home. If I could reach through this phone, I'd slap your face."

I hung up and made a mental note to call the Gas Department first thing in the morning.

ON MY OWN
19

Although Philadelphia was eight hundred miles away, Rick would be home every weekend . . . at least in theory. In spite of our careful planning, we forgot one minor detail: we don't control the weather.

"The weather reports say this could be the worst snow storm to hit the area in over a decade," Rick informed me on the phone one evening. "We already have nine inches, and it's still coming down. They just announced the airport is closing. I'm afraid I won't be coming home this weekend."

Two weeks had passed since saying goodbye to Rick and leaving Philadelphia. We both agreed he should spend his first weekend settling into his new job, but the onslaught of this blizzard meant yet another week would go by before he made it home. I began wondering if we would ever see him again.

Our first weekend apart was one I will never forget. Saturday started out well enough. In fact, I rather enjoyed operating on my own schedule. It snowed that day, and I raised the shades throughout the house to take full advantage of the view.

Kathryn went to bed early, but I found it hard to fall asleep without Rick, so I stayed up to tackle the Christmas decorations. Our trip to Philadelphia prevented their prompt removal, and our neighbors were dropping not-so-subtle hints about their lingering presence. One neighbor volunteered her teenage son to help take down the wreaths on our windows. Another applauded my ingenuity in turning our Christmas lights into year-round decor.

I made some hot chocolate, popped *Miracle on 34th Street* into the VCR and started taking down our tree. Nine boxes and three garbage bags later, I called it quits and went upstairs.

I glanced at the clock beside my bed and was surprised to see it was after one o'clock. I changed into my nightgown and crawled in bed but then remembered I had forgotten to check the locks. I made my way back downstairs and after confirming the house was secure, paused at a window to look out at the snow. Something in the distance caught my attention. I stared into the darkness and a moment later saw the unmistakable glow of a cigarette. Someone was in our backyard watching our house.

Panic surged through my body like lightning. My heart pounded as I ran upstairs and peeked out the bathroom window. There it was again. Someone was out there. What did they want? Did they know I was alone with Kathryn? Were they planning to break in the house once they thought I was asleep? I ran to the phone and dialed 911. My hand was shaking so hard it was difficult to hold the receiver to my ear.

The minute someone answered, I blurted, "Please help. I'm alone with my daughter, and there's someone watching our house."

"Don't panic. I have your address, and I'm notifying the police right now. They should be at your house in less than ten minutes. Stay on the line until they arrive."

A moment later, our doorbell rang. I looked out and was relieved to find two police officers standing on the porch.

"Thank goodness you're here. Someone is standing in our backyard watching the house. I looked out just a few minutes ago, and he was still there."

"Stay inside and keep the doors locked. We'll take a look around the house. If someone is out there, it shouldn't be hard to track him in the snow. Remember, don't unlock the door unless you're sure it's one of us."

They left, and I secured the door. It wasn't long before there was another knock. I looked out and saw both officers.

"Did you find anyone? Did you see any tracks?" I asked.

"Yes, ma'am. We found tracks in your backyard and followed them to a home on the other side of the cul-de-sac. The teenager who lives there is having a slumber party, and he and his friends slipped out for a smoke. He picked your backyard because it's not visible from his house. We spoke with his parents, and I don't think it will happen again."

I thanked the officers and trudged back upstairs. It was a relief to know Jack the Ripper wasn't in the backyard. Those juvenile delinquents had nearly given me a heart attack. When I reached the top of the stairs, Kathryn's door opened.

"What's going on? I thought I heard someone talking."

I gave her a quick play-by-play of the past hour.

"Oh," she said before making her way back to bed.

I sat down on the top step and rested my head in my hands. It was after three o'clock, and I hadn't managed even five minutes of sleep. I took a deep breath and exhaled. It was time to face reality: I had a husband who lived eight hundred miles away and a teenage daughter focused on her own life, not mine. There were seven hundred and nine days to go in our adventure, and I had to find a way to get through them – alone.

"How many tickets did you say?" asked the US Airways representative on the phone.

"Ten. I need to buy one round trip ticket for each of ten different weekends."

Reserving discounted airline tickets, coordinating calendars three months in advance and struggling to maintain some semblance of family life became the center of my existence. It was exhausting trying to juggle our schedules.

Rick did his best to make it home on weekends, but more often than not, the weather or his job made it impossible. By the time his second year at Penn rolled around, he was seldom at home. Even worse, he was never in my thoughts. It wasn't unusual to make plans and then realize I had forgotten to include him. The distance between us took its toll, and he slowly became little more than an afterthought in my life.

When Kathryn's senior year began, so did the deluge of college applications in our mailbox. After meeting Amy Calhoun, Penn's most gregarious and captivating admissions officer, her heart was set on Penn. She was convinced no school in the nation could match its audacious spirit or offer its myriad opportunities. She was right, but I still insisted she come up with a list of other schools to consider. When Rick first arrived at Penn, it ranked sixteenth among national universities. Two years later, it moved up to number seven. Change of this magnitude, in such a short amount of time, was unheard of in academia. With the possible exception of eighteen-year-old prodigies, it was no one's safety school.

In the fall, Rick accompanied Kathryn and me on a tour of colleges in the northeast. It was imperative for her to identify at least a few other schools in which to apply. Our first stop was Boston University. An information session for prospective students and their parents had scarcely begun when Kathryn leaned over and whispered, "I'm not applying here."

"You haven't even heard the speaker."

"It doesn't matter. Do you see what those tour guides are wearing? Blazers. They're wearing blazers."

"They're just wearing them to differentiate themselves on the tour."

"It doesn't matter. I won't consider any university that requires anyone to wear a blazer under any circumstance."

We got up and left the room.

Our next stop was Tufts University. We made it through the information session, but as everyone fell in line for the campus tour, Kathryn motioned for us to step aside.

"We can go now. I've seen enough," she said.

"What do you mean 'you've seen enough'? The only thing we've seen is the inside of a lecture hall."

"Did you notice anything about the speaker?"

"Not in particular. What are you referring to?"

"Coughing. He coughed the entire time. It was so annoying. There's something about this whole place that annoys me."

We turned and made our way back to the car.

Our final destination that day was Haverford College. Haverford is an excellent school located right outside of Philadelphia. If my research was correct, it might be the perfect fit for Kathryn.

The information session went well. The speaker was articulate, entertaining and didn't cough a single time. I breathed a sigh of relief when the meeting ended and I realized we were going on the campus tour. An hour later, we thanked our tour guide and headed for the car.

"So, what do you think?" I asked.

"I like it, but I wouldn't come here for college."

"Why not?" Rick asked.

"Do you remember what the tour guide said when we were in the student center?"

"Not exactly."

"He said there's an honor code on campus, and if you forget your backpack and leave it on the floor, it will be there when you get back. In the real world, if you leave your bag, someone is going to take it. I want a college that prepares me for the world, not one that shelters me from it."

As we strolled back to the car, I put my arm around her shoulder. I didn't always agree with her decisions, but she knew her own mind. That's a valuable asset in the real world.

A few days later, she dropped her application to Penn in the mail, and we all held our breath.

THE CREST OF THE MOUNTAIN 20

Our last Christmas in Nashville came and went. I watched as Rick shoved our holiday decorations through the small opening into the attic. Before long, he would be bringing them down again.

"Is that it? Are we finished?" he asked.

"Yes. That's the last box."

"You'll have fun finding places for everything to go in the new house next Christmas," he said.

I turned away and began picking up stray bits of tinsel from the carpet. I wished some of Rick's holiday cheer would wear off on me. Packing our decorations only reminded me of our upcoming move to Philadelphia and all the changes about to take place.

I had two years to prepare, yet I had done nothing to get ready. I had convinced myself this move would never happen. My state of denial came at a high cost, not the least of which was my marriage.

In spite of giving Rick my support to go to Penn, I now resented having to leave the life I built in Nashville. I knew my feelings were sabotaging our happiness, but I couldn't let go of my anger. Although shameful and unfair, something inside me wanted him to hurt the way I did.

We planned to put our home on the market in late spring and move to Philadelphia by midsummer. I was on the phone speaking with a real estate agent one afternoon when I heard a scream come from the front yard.

"I'll have to call you back," I said before hanging up.

I raced to the front door as Kathryn ran up the driveway.

"I made it!" she shouted. "I'm going to Penn!"

Kathryn bounded up the porch steps and handed me the letter she had just plucked from our mailbox.

"On behalf of the entire Penn community, it gives me great pleasure to . . ."

I dropped the letter and threw my arms around her.

"Call Dad! He'll be so excited."

Unfortunately, Rick was in a meeting, and Kathryn was told he couldn't be interrupted. The smile on her face disappeared, and my heart ached. Another important moment would go unshared between them. We were unaware Rick's assistant realized the importance of Kathryn's call and slipped him a note. As he unfolded the message, he read *Congratulations. You're a Penn Parent.* It was less than five minute before he phoned.

"So you did it. You tricked Penn into admitting you," he said.

They spoke for a long time, and I smiled listening to the laughter interspersed in their conversation. We had arrived at the crest of a mountain we had struggled to climb and found a gift waiting for us – Kathryn was coming to Philadelphia.

"Dad wants to talk to you."

Kathryn tossed me the phone before running upstairs.

"So, how do feel about the news?" Rick asked.

"I think it's the best gift anyone ever gave me."

"I'm glad. You deserve to feel that way. You've been a terrific mother."

My eyes swelled with tears. No one needed to tell Rick how much he had missed. He knew. We had all sacrificed too much for too long.

"I don't know how you got through the last two years. At least Kathryn and I had each other."

"And now, we'll all be together again. It's what I've wished for ever since I got here."

"You spent two years wishing for something you already had?"

The phone was silent and I thought the line was dead.

"Rick, are you there?"

"I didn't spend the last two years wishing I could change the decision we made. I spent them realizing what it cost us."

Our marriage endured the hardest test it ever faced, and our commitment and love matured in ways only adversity can teach. We remembered what loneliness felt like, and neither of us ever wanted to experience it again.

As the end of the school year approached, I began planning in earnest for our move to Philadelphia. I selected a realtor, hired a moving company and created a detailed spreadsheet on what went where and when. Unfortunately, things on Rick's end moved a lot slower.

The real estate agent Rick selected in Philadelphia came highly recommended by a colleague at Penn. A mature, older woman with impeccable manners, style and pedigree, *Constance* was a bona fide member of the Merion Cricket Club. In other words, she was a true daughter of the Main Line.

The Main Line. Just the thought of it conjures up memories of picturesque village squares anchored by old-fashioned train stations. Only on the Main Line do seasons of the year compete to outdo one another in beauty. Springtime plays host to enormous rhododendrons bursting forth in color on lush lawns and in manicured parks. Only clear blue skies and warm breezes are permitted on summer days. In the fall, leaves of brilliant crimson, gold and orange adorn each roadway, and as the air grows cold and winter arrives, the first snow waits patiently until Christmas Eve to blanket the ground in shimmering white.

Before moving to Philadelphia, I was unfamiliar with its affluent western suburbs. In the 19th century, when the Pennsylvania Railroad connected the city of Philadelphia to these small towns, wealthy families rushed to the region to build lavish country estates. The Main Line was, and is, a bastion of old money in the northeast.

We had less than two months to find a new home in Philadelphia, yet Constance refused to acknowledge the urgency of our situation. I surmised selling real estate might be no more than a hobby for her and that Rick was uncomfortable making demands. Eventually, weary of my nagging, he took control and persuaded her to commit an entire weekend to showing us properties for sale in the area. I flew up on a Friday night determined to return to Nashville with a signed contract on a house.

We met Constance at her club Saturday morning at ten o'clock to discuss current real estate trends and consume mouth-watering croissants. She took a sip of coffee, dabbed her perfectly lined lips with a cloth napkin and looked me over. I felt like Eliza Doolittle being scrutinized by the great Professor Henry Higgins in *My Fair Lady* and wondered how short I fell of her expectations. Apparently, pretty far because she soon launched into a litany of fashion advice.

"Dear, one thing to remember is never wear your tennis whites anywhere other than your club. To do so is quite a *faux pas*."

My tennis whites? I hadn't played tennis since college, and even then, my attire consisted of a tee shirt and a pair of shorts with a peace symbol on the back pocket. Tips on the social etiquette of the Main Line would have to wait. We needed a home. I shifted the topic of conversation to an issue more critical than my future wardrobe requirements.

"How many houses have you arranged for us to tour today?" I asked.

"I believe we have three homes to inspect."

"Only three? Aren't there others we can see? This is my only chance to be in Philadelphia for the next four weeks."

"There's no reason for concern, dear. I'm sure one of these will be appropriate."

Rick gave me his "I told you so" look. Nonetheless, I intended to push the envelope until I had seen everything available.

"We'll begin with homes on the Main Line. There's no reason to search elsewhere unless we're absolutely forced to do so," Constance said.

I didn't care where we went, as long as we started looking.

We left the club at eleven o'clock for our first appointment. I knew the moment we got there it was the wrong house for us. It was a three-story stone colonial with a circular driveway. I expected a butler to emerge at any moment to open our car doors.

"Is this house in our price range?" I asked.

"Heavens, no. I just want you to have a flavor for what's available at different prices."

I hurried us through the house and back to the front door.

"Are you sure you gave this house the proper assessment it deserves?" Constance asked.

"It's a beautiful home, but I think we should concentrate our efforts on houses within our price range. I'm afraid we don't have time to see houses other than those we can afford."

"Of course, we'll do whatever you prefer, dear. However, as a rule, the more knowledgeable one is of the total housing market, the wiser one's judgment is when it comes time to extend an offer."

Was I mistaken, or did she just imply that I was foolish? Eloquence can make things so hard to interpret.

Our next stop was Villanova. The word *small* would be vastly over-stating the proportions of the house we were about to tour. The tiny doors and windows baffled me. I couldn't imagine how an ordinary person could live there.

"This house is so small," I said.

"That's because it's not a real house," Constance answered.

I gazed at her with a blank expression and restrained myself from asking the obvious.

"It's the original gatehouse for the estate down the driveway. In spite of that, it's entirely appropriate."

Appropriate for whom? A family of dwarves? A quick glance down the driveway revealed yet another three-story stone colonial with a circular driveway.

"There's no need to spend time here. I don't think Rick or our belongings will fit well in such a small place."

"If you're sure that's what you want, dear."

If she called me *dear* just once more, I thought I might jump out of her new BMW. Rick sensed I was at my boiling point and tried to salvage the situation.

"Constance, I think we're looking for something sort of in-between the types of houses you've shown us," he said.

That's right, I thought, something smaller than a palace but larger than a box. My frustration escalated into despair. If our pace didn't pick up soon, we would never find a house this weekend. I took a deep breath and tried to refocus.

Before long, we entered a gated community of about fifty houses. They were relatively new – a rarity on the Main Line. Constance pulled in the driveway of a lovely two-story house with lots of curb appeal. We thought it might be perfect for us until we went inside.

158

The first thing we noticed was the lack of doorknobs. There wasn't a single doorknob in the entire house. Who could live in a house with no doorknobs? After further examination, a number of other flaws became apparent. There were cracks in the walls of the master bedroom, none of the ceiling fans worked, mold had taken over both showers and there was not a single exterior light.

When we mentioned our concerns to Constance, her only reaction was a dispassionate "Oh, my." Was there a chance the sellers might adjust the price? Constance told us not to count on it.

"People on the Main Line aren't accustomed to haggling over the price of their property. Asking sellers to make allowances can be extremely upsetting."

I suggested we leave and continue our search. Rick didn't agree.

"I'm afraid it will only get worse. I've looked at over a hundred houses, and this is the best one I've seen," Rick said.

We resigned ourselves to our fate and asked Constance to prepare an offer. After arranging to meet with her the following morning, we left.

"Don't worry. Before you know it, we'll have the house in good condition and feeling like home," Rick said.

We met Constance at her office the next morning.

"Today is your big day," she said smiling. "I have the offer ready to present, and I've arranged for us to meet with the sellers' agent at ten o'clock. Are you ready?"

I cringed as I climbed into the back seat of her car. My disappointed stemmed from more than just the condition of the house. This day marked the beginning of our new life in Philadelphia, and I wanted it to be a happy time. Constance noticed our silence and glum expressions.

"If I'm not mistaken, I don't think either of you genuinely likes the house you've chosen. May I suggest you see one other property before we present your offer? A home in Bryn Mawr just came on the market today, and the owners are holding an open house. Shall we take a look?"

Rick turned toward me. We had waited a long time for this day to arrive. We hadn't shared a home together in over two years.

"We don't have anything to lose," he said.

He asked Constance to drive us by the house. In all honesty, I don't think either of us expected to find something we liked waiting for us in Bryn Mawr. It was just a way of postponing the decision we had made the day before.

"Here we are," Constance said pulling to the curb. "What do you think?"

I was engrossed in my thoughts and unaware the car had stopped. I turned and casually looked out the window. When I did, my eyes fell on a quaint two-story colonial house covered in Pennsylvania stone.

"I love it!"

As soon as I uttered the words, I regretted them. The house looked expensive and the last thing I wanted was for Rick to think the house we had already chosen was my second choice. As if he were reading my thoughts, he said, "It's all right. I feel the same way."

"Isn't it charming? I've played bridge here on numerous occasions so I am quite familiar with the floor plan. It's a lovely home with recently updated bathrooms and kitchen."

"We both like the house, but it looks expensive. If we can't afford it, I'd rather not go inside," I said.

"Wait here while I check on the price."

Constance left the car and went inside. I looked at Rick. We both seemed to be holding our breath. Constance was inside quite a while before coming back to the car.

"The house was indeed out of your price range. However, when I told the sellers, who are both friends of mine, I had buyers ready to sign a contract, they decided to reduce the sale price to match your offer on the other house. In fact, they agreed to a little less. I'm afraid I had a slight memory loss when I gave them the figure."

I hugged Constance and thanked her profusely. I had sorely underestimated her intellect and ingenuity. She deserved more respect. I bet if you took away her Louis Vuitton wallet, the Cartier bracelet hanging from her wrist, the Gucci sunglasses shielding her eyes and the Prada bag flung casually over her shoulder, she'd be just like the rest of us.

I flew home the next day, clutching a copy of the contract on our new house. It was time to turn up the heat. With the closing date set on the house in Bryn Mawr, the time had come to put our home on the market. Kathryn and I watched our realtor hammer a *for sale* sign into our front yard a few days later.

"The house is in excellent condition. It'll sell in no time," our agent said.

She was right. It sold the day it went on the market to the first people who looked at it.

There was no turning back.

The end of May arrived, and with it came Kathryn's high school graduation. Our families gathered at our house to celebrate on the day of the ceremony. It was a bittersweet time. A chapter in my life was ending, and I wasn't ready. I still had valuable information to share with my daughter – not to mention at least a dozen unspoken lectures. The years had passed too quickly. I still had warnings to issue and advice to offer. Most of all, I wanted to know I had done my job well.

As Kathryn walked across the stage, she flashed us a bright smile and waved. Rick reached for my hand. Neither of us spoke, but I knew we were both thinking the same thing. Somehow, in spite of all our missteps, our daughter had managed to turn out just fine.

I thought of the words spoken to me eighteen years ago as I left the hospital, "Don't worry, she's a lot tougher than she looks."

The nurse was right.

YO! PHILLY

21

I opened another box and discovered more baby clothes and toys. Why had I kept all this stuff? A second child hadn't been on our wish list in years. After numerous failed attempts, we called it quits. Once we reached that decision, avoiding a pregnancy became our singular goal in life. Overnight I went from monitoring my temperature and frequenting the offices of infertility specialists to abstaining from sex and anything that came close to resembling it.

The moving van would be here in just three weeks, and clearing out the attic was number one on my checklist. It was ridiculous to continue storing all these baby items. I needed to go through each box, save one or two items of sentimental value and donate everything else to Goodwill.

I opened one of the boxes and looked inside. Laying on top of a soft blue blanket that once hung meticulously on the end of Kathryn's crib was a small yellow duck. I could picture Kathryn at age two, laughing as I dropped it into her bathwater and yelled, "Geronimo!" I closed the box and pushed it aside. I repeated this action numerous times, and after an hour, the only thing I had discarded was a plastic pumpkin Kathryn once used for trick-or-treating.

Just when another wave of moving anxiety was about to hit me, I remembered our new house in Bryn Mawr had a huge attic. I could wait and sort through everything after the move! I took out my checklist and drew a line through *clean out the attic.*

Sleeping pills were the next item on my list—not for me—for our pets. With an eight hundred mile drive looming before us, thoughts of being held hostage to a hyperactive collie and a calico cat that harbored an unexplained grudge against all of us left me no option but narcotics. I phoned our veterinarian and explained the situation.

"No problem. I know those animals. The drugs will be waiting for you at the front desk," he said.

Three weeks later, I stood at an upstairs window and watched the truck parked at the end of our driveway. The movers had spent the past two days packing and loading all of our belongings into the van. After the first day, I asked if they could leave our beds in the house so we could spend our last night there. It was a request I always regretted. Nothing feels lonelier than sleeping in an empty house that was once your home.

The movers arrived early the next day to finish loading. While they hoisted our beds onto the van, I used the opportunity to walk through our home one last time. I checked every cabinet, drawer and closet. Everything was empty. The movers left nothing behind, but we did. Everywhere I looked, I found something we were leaving behind . . . some visible reminder this house had been our home. The charcoal stains on the patio? They were the result of Rick's overzealous attempt to master the art of grilling. The bits of masking tape on the walls in Kathryn's bedroom? Clues to where a poster of the *New Kids on the Block* and signs from the Clinton/ Gore campaign once hung. The chunks of concrete missing from the driveway outside the garage door? When a winter storm hit our area a few years back, I warned Rick what would happen if he used a shovel to break up the ice. There was a story behind everything. Stories only we knew and would never forget.

Rick loaded our luggage in the car while I administered the sleeping pills to both pets. As our car pulled out of the driveway, Kathryn turned and took one last look at the house she would forever call home. Rick tried to be inconspicuous, but I saw him glance in the rear view mirror. I kept my eyes on the road ahead, determined not to look back.

When the Nashville skyline came in sight, I reached for Rick's hand. After seven hundred and thirty days, one journey was ending and another about to begin. We turned east on Interstate 40. Philadelphia was our next stop on the road of life.

"Stop it!"

I was dozing, and Kathryn's scream sent my heart racing. I looked in the back seat just in time to catch a glimpse of our collie, Rhett Butler, licking the mirror in front of him. We had been on the road to Philadelphia for seven long hours, and both pets had recovered from their drug-induced sleep.

The mirror Kathryn was trying to protect had belonged to my grandmother. I have fond memories of watching her sit before it while she combed her beautiful silver hair. It was now wedged between Kathryn's knees and the front seat, an unexpected addition to our already over-stuffed car. We forgot to have it crated, and the movers explained it was far too old and delicate for the moving van. Sadly, it was not faring much better in the back seat of our car.

"Kathryn, please control Rhett Butler. We put the mirror in the car so it would be in good shape when we got to Philly. If he destroys it before we get there, what was the point of taking up all your space in the back seat?"

Kathryn rolled her eyes and picked up a towel to remove Rhett's drool from the mirror. I noticed when it was clean, she used the opportunity to examine her face - again. For a self-conscious eighteen-year-old girl about to start college, the mirror provided relentless enticement to scrutinize every inch of her appearance.

I sighed, reached in my purse and took out the bottle of prescription sleeping pills that had gotten us through the past seven hours. I leaned over the front seat, grabbed both pets by the scruff of their necks and pushed the pills down their throats. Within minutes, the car was quiet, and peace returned to the back seat. Seven hours down and six to go.

Two things come to mind when I think of the summer we moved to Philadelphia. First, we arrived in the early morning hours of July 4, a perfect day to become official residents of the city that gave birth to our country. Second, it was the summer of Clinton and Lewinsky.

My uncanny ability to recall every minute detail of the Clinton/Lewinsky scandal is due primarily to the unique circumstances surrounding our living arrangements that summer. Although we agreed to give the buyers of our Nashville home possession by July 3, we were unable to move into our new home in Bryn Mawr until early October. We were therefore fated to spend the summer in Rick's six hundred square foot apartment in the not-so-quaint Old Quaker. Additionally, the beginning of Penn's fall semester and Kathryn's move into campus housing would occur in September, which meant all her dorm furnishings and college supplies would have to follow us into apartment 2D.

Given our cramped living quarters, it would have been preferable to spend as much time as possible outdoors. However, these were the months of July and August, and this was the city of Philadelphia - a place known for its blistering summer heat and hellish humidity. Both conditions kept us sequestered within the air-conditioned confines of the apartment. In spite of limited internet access, we tried to entertain ourselves with our new computer and our television.

Thus began the season of Clinton and Lewinsky.

Our forty-second President's reputation as a serial philanderer preceded him to the Oval Office. In spite of this, when news broke of his alleged misconduct with a young White House intern named Monica Lewinsky, most of the country seemed willing to accept his denial. In a televised broadcast from the White House on January 26, 1998, Clinton pointed his finger at us and declared, "I did not have sexual relations with that woman, Miss Lewinsky." From that point on, it was downhill for Bill.

Week after week, commentators discussed and dissected our President's exploits. Pieced together, they painted a rather explicit picture. The question of *what to do about Bill* became the topic of conversation everywhere. I spent half my time trying to catch the news and the other half trying to hide it from Kathryn. As it turned out, it was a pointless effort. A year later, she served as an intern in the Clinton White House and made frequent trips to and from Betty Currie's desk right outside the Oval Office.

I was determined to get Kathryn out of the apartment and involved in something more productive than chronicling Bill Clinton's exploits. After asking around, I learned Penn's new bookstore needed help preparing for their grand opening in late August. The bookstore was Barnes and Noble's first attempt at a joint business arrangement to operate a college bookstore. It would anchor the first phase of a complex of buildings known as Sansom Common and was the Trustees' first step in revitalizing the area surrounding Penn's campus. Best of all, it was only two short blocks from the Old Quaker.

Recruiting employees for the bookstore was harder than anyone expected. The number of applicants was weak, and those who did apply lacked basic skills. Rick convinced Kathryn helping with the opening of the bookstore would be a worthwhile use of her time while also earning cash for the fall. She grudgingly filled out an application, interviewed for a job and began working all on the same day. Over the course of the next three weeks, she rose from being a file clerk in the Department of Human

Resources to screening job applicants and making hiring decisions. Lest she become arrogant due to her rapid advancement, Rick reminded her the bookstore was desperate.

Kathryn returned to the apartment one afternoon and discovered an email from her future freshman roommate, Suzanne. Suzie, as we came to know her, had taken the initiative to contact Kathryn and introduce herself. She was from Scarsdale, an affluent suburb of New York City. She was Jewish, attended one of the best public high schools in the country and summered in Maine at Camp Walden. Camp Walden is a highly regarded camp for girls offering activities such as horseback riding, tennis, sailing and water skiing.

In contrast, Kathryn was from Nashville (a.k.a. Music City U.S.A.). She was Christian, attended a private high school suffering from lukewarm academics, and spent two weeks each summer at Brevard Music Center. Brevard is a remote camp in North Carolina that offers private music instruction, practice in group performance and weekend trips to the local Walmart. I silently wondered how Kathryn would measure up to her new classmates.

September marked the start of move-in for Penn freshmen, and Kathryn and Suzie were ecstatic about their assignment to a dorm room in Penn's Quadrangle. Known affectionately as *the Quad*, this collection of historic buildings has been the residence of choice for Penn's freshmen since 1895. A quick walk-through reveals few renovations have occurred since then, but in spite of its disrepair, the Quad remains the hub of action for freshmen. It was into this action-packed firetrap of a building we prepared to move our only child.

Kathryn used fifty dollars of her summer earnings from the bookstore to take advantage of the early move-in option. She surmised this would allow her to choose the most desirable side of the room (as if either side of a 150-year-old unrenovated room could possibly be *desirable)*. I was amazed at the speed with which my once thoughtful and generous daughter acquired Yankee ingenuity, otherwise known as "me first syndrome." Such bold posturing would serve her well one day, but for now, it just seemed selfish.

We made trip after trip between the Quad and the apartment. Drawers on wheels, posters of the Beatles, a denim comforter, her stuffed lobster from Bar Harbor and way too many clothes for her tiny closet were all transported that day. At four o'clock, we dragged our hot, weary bodies back to the air-conditioned comfort of the Old Quaker. We were relaxing while consuming tall glasses of ice-cold water when Kathryn made her move, quite literally, out of our home forever.

"Mom and Dad, it's time for me to leave."

I was unable to speak. My mouth couldn't form a single word. Why didn't she just cut my heart out? It would have been preferable to hearing my own child, the baby once handed to me in a soft yellow blanket, announce she was done with me. She was leaving. She kissed both of us gently on the cheek, picked up her backpack, turned and walked out the door. Rick and I stared at each other as if someone had just announced the world was ending and we could do nothing about it.

I went to the bedroom and flung myself on the bed. Between sobs, I became aware of something hitting the window next to me. I looked out and saw my newly empowered daughter standing on the corner of 36th Street and Lancaster Avenue throwing pebbles at the window. She had been gone a total of two minutes.

I called Rick, and he joined me at the window. Kathryn waved goodbye and began her six-block journey to independence. At that moment, it occurred to me distance alone did not make one nest any emptier than another did. Like an unused chair at the table or a bed no longer slept in, an empty space is an empty space.

No one warned me how painful saying goodbye would be. I suppose, similar to bringing your first child home from the hospital, no one can truly prepare you for the experience. For me, it was a time of deep reflection on what was, what could have been and what was no longer possible.

As we watched Kathryn disappear down Lancaster Avenue, neither of us spoke. There was no need; we both understood what the other felt. There are times when words cannot match what the heart feels, and this was one of them. Just a few hours later, however, Kathryn phoned. She discovered there were drawbacks to early move-in: she was the only person on her floor.

"Would it be all right if I slept at the Old Quaker tonight?" she asked.

She had been gone two hours and was already coming home. This was my introduction to the rhythm of life I shared with my daughter for the next ten years. Like Houdini, she was there one moment and gone the next.

Penn's Class of 2002, with its average SAT score of 1401, was the most selective class in Penn's history. Knowledge of this mental aptitude was unknown to me when I accepted Professor Jim O'Donnell's invitation to serve as a discussion leader for the Penn Reading Project.

The book chosen for the Class of 2002 was Maxine Hong Kingston's *The Woman Warrior*. Freshmen were required to read the memoir before arriving on campus and participate in a discussion group during orientation.

Penn literature describes the Penn Reading Project as the first opportunity for freshmen to engage in serious intellectual discourse on a topic of current or historical interest. Unfortunately, for these rising stars of academia, *I* would be leading their first serious intellectual discussion. If I had had any pride, I would have surrendered my role to someone better qualified to fill it. However, enjoying a challenge the way I do, I bought a copy of the book and dug in.

As it turned out, my apprehension was unnecessary. I was spared the embarrassment of my inferior intellect because the students assigned to my discussion group were too intimidated by each other to speak. I presented a brief analysis of the book and asked if there were any questions. There was only one, and no one could answer it, so I suggested we dismiss early and research the topic.

I left the lecture hall and hurried to Professor O'Donnell's on-campus apartment for his celebratory cocktail party. In due course, I consumed one too many glasses of chardonnay and told Jim (at least I think I did) under no circumstances would I ever serve as a discussion leader again. Penn was becoming more selective every year, and eventually, someone would call my bluff.

The following night was Convocation - the first time the freshman class marches together. The procession winds its way through campus and ends in front of College Hall, home to the office of Penn's president. It was there Dr. Rodin planned to address the class and officially welcome them into the Penn community.

I learned about this opening ceremony with a mixture of curiosity and envy. Convocation was a novel concept to me. No one shook my hand or wished me good luck when I began classes. We just turned to page one in our textbooks and started reading. Kathryn phoned on Friday to remind me Convocation began at six-thirty.

"You'll be there, won't you?" she asked.

"Of course. You might not see me, but I'll be there."

I left the apartment a little after six o'clock and headed down 36th Street. The moment I entered the campus, I found myself engulfed in a bustle of activity. I watched for Kathryn as the Class of 2002 marched down Locust Walk, the main thoroughfare of campus. I soon spotted her in a group of smiling faces that included her roommate Suzie. When she and

Kathryn finally met, they hit it off immediately. The differences in their backgrounds only served to enrich their relationship.

The students took their seats in front of College Hall as President Rodin gave a short but deeply inspiring introduction to Penn. Rick was obligated to march in Convocation, so we didn't have the opportunity to talk until later that night.

"I learned something tonight," I said.

We were lying on the couch listening to my favorite classical CD. Rhett Butler lay curled up on the floor beside us snoring softly. We hadn't seen the cat in days, but knew he was there somewhere.

"What did you learn?" Rick asked.

"I learned no matter where we are, as long as we're together, I can be happy."

"Let's make a deal right now that we'll never be separated again and that only one of us can go crazy at a time," Rick said.

"Sounds good to me."

"When do I get my turn?" Rick asked.

"What turn?"

"My turn to go crazy."

"Someday . . . when everything is calm, and our lives are in order."

He smiled, and I knew why. Things would never calm down, and our lives would never be in order. He had no hope of ever getting a turn.

PRECONCEIVED NOTIONS 22

I woke the next morning to the intoxicating aroma of freshly brewed coffee but discovered Rick had emptied the pot. I searched for more, but we were out. In the past, this would represent nothing more than a minor annoyance. It now, however, created quite a dilemma because restocking the coffee meant a trip to the Seven Eleven.

Rick and I developed the habit of renting a car on weekends and roaming around the area where we would soon be living. Before returning to the city, we always stopped at one of the well-stocked markets on the Main Line and bought our groceries for the coming week. Unfortunately, this past week, we had forgotten to put coffee on our list.

I could manage to control my caffeine addiction for one or two days, but not all week. That's where the Seven Eleven came in. It was the only nearby option for purchasing coffee. I avoided going there whenever possible because the business transactions that took place right outside its doors were hard to ignore; for the right price, a person could acquire just about anything he or she wanted. Nonetheless, with my hands trembling from caffeine withdrawal, I grabbed my purse and headed out the door.

The neighborhood surrounding the Old Quaker intrigued me. Half of the buildings were abandoned, and the others buzzed with non-stop activity. I found two places across the street especially compelling - a fencing school and a restaurant.

The sign hanging above the school read, "The Fencing Academy of Philadelphia: Beginner to World Champion." I liked their confidence. It takes nerve to promise something like that. Their additional advertising, however, left me uneasy.

"Make friends with people of all ages via the intensity of armed combat."

I will admit making new friends can be difficult, but resorting to warfare as a means of social networking seemed rather desperate.

Mad Greek's Pizza sits across from the Old Quaker. At first glance, it appears to be just another dingy hole-in-the-wall eatery. However, the cars lined up outside its doors at all hours of the day and night made us suspect something other than food might be for sale. It took over a month for us to work up the courage to cross the street and check it out. When we did, we learned it was famous for having the best pizza in the city. They also serve cheese steaks, hoagies, wraps and gyros. I had no idea what a gyro was but was too intimidated to ask.

I finally arrived at the Seven Eleven and was thankful to get in and out without incident. On a prior visit, I was propositioned and cursed. Both were a high price to pay for a gallon of milk.

As much as I hated going to the Seven Eleven, I was grateful for its presence. It was the only place within walking distance to buy groceries. When I became a resident of Philadelphia, the insurance on my red Mitsubishi convertible rose from six hundred dollars a year to over two thousand. Rick sold it before I even had time to clean out the glove box.

The most difficult part of urban living was getting from one place to another. During my first week in Philadelphia, I visited the Reading Terminal Market, an extraordinary marketplace filled with every type of food imaginable. Fresh produce, delicious breads made by the local Amish community, seafood, meats of every description, it is all there under one roof.

I strolled leisurely up and down each aisle before selecting a bundle of fresh vegetables, a jar of homemade jam, a mouth-watering blueberry pie and two enormous chickens. When the butcher handed me my purchase, I realized how burdensome my packages had become. No problem, I would just take a cab back to the Old Quaker.

Unfortunately, when I reached in my purse to ensure I had the fare, I discovered I had spent all my cash at the market. The apartment was too far away to walk, and my shopping bags were already digging trenches in my arms. I was racking my brain for a solution when I caught sight of a city bus headed in my direction. I rummaged through my purse and found a token. The joy of my discovery created a sensation similar to striking gold.

The bus pulled up, and I climbed aboard. I groaned when I realized there were no empty seats. Left with no choice, I positioned myself behind the driver, wedged the bag of chickens between my feet and spaced the plastic bags up and down my forearms.

We made good progress until the stop at 30th Street Station. When the door opened, a woman with long unkempt hair mounted the stairs. Her eyes darted about as if they were simultaneously focusing on everything and nothing. Although it was July and over ninety degrees, she was dressed in a thick gray sweater.

The woman's difficulty climbing the steps was heart wrenching, but what happened next was even more alarming. As she topped the stairs, she lunged forward to grab hold of the coin deposit box. She clung to it for support as she mumbled to the driver, "I got to get to da hospital."

"This bus don't go to the hospital. You gotta take the Seven."

"They won't take me 'cause I don't got no money."

"I can't do nothing about that. If you don't got the fare, you have to get off the bus."

I was appalled. The poor woman was obviously in need of help. Why didn't the driver call for assistance? I looked around and saw no one was even paying attention. The man across the aisle continued to read his newspaper; the woman behind him did not skip a beat in her cell phone conversation; and the people up front, occupying the handicapped seats, kept dozing. Was I the only person aware of what was happening? Didn't anyone care? I wanted to help, but all I could offer was a chicken, veggies, jam or a pie.

The driver's exchange with the woman seemed to go on forever. I leaned forward trying to reduce the strain on my back and noticed the bag holding my chickens had begun to leak. Blood was pooling on the floor and streaming down the aisle. I tried to look as if I had no idea whose chickens they were or where they had come from, despite the fact they were lodged between my feet.

Someone yelled, "How long we gonna sit here? Either let her on or put her off!"

A man seated about midway down the aisle stood up and offered to give the woman money for a cab. I fought the urge to inquire if he might also have enough to get me back to the Old Quaker. We passed the cash up the aisle and into the hands of the woman.

"God bless you," she cried.

The poor woman descended the steps, and the bus pulled away from the curb.

"Next stop is 34th Street," the driver calmly announced in the loudspeaker.

His composure amazed me. He acted as if this sort of thing happened every day.

It took a week for the marks left behind by my shopping bags to fade from my arms and even longer for the image of that sad, impoverished woman to disappear from my thoughts. The generosity of the man who volunteered cab fare surprised me. Yet, while living in Philadelphia, I observed similar acts of compassion dozens of times, in various places and often by the least likely person. Day by day, my prejudice and preconceived notions about people began to change.

Urban life opened my eyes to many things, some good and some not, but overall, the lessons I came away with reinforced my belief that most of us try to help each other out.

Living in the Old Quaker gave me the opportunity to experience city life in all its dimensions. However, it was a fleeting exercise. Within a few months, we were back in the sanctuary of the suburbs.

FIRST AND LAST IMPRESSIONS 23

I stood in the front yard of our new home in Bryn Mawr as one of the movers lay the wing of an angel in my hands. She was part of a celestial statue that once guarded our home in Nashville. Now it and my favorite birdbath were headed for the dump. It seemed odd that of all the fragile items placed inside the moving van, only two objects, both made of solid concrete, failed to survive the journey northward.

Early that morning, we packed our suitcases and said goodbye to the Old Quaker. I noticed Rick didn't look back when we pulled out of the parking lot. We arrived in Bryn Mawr ahead of the movers and used the opportunity to snap a few photos of the house. We secured Rhett Butler in one of the bathrooms, but when I took the cat out of his crate, he hissed, scratched me across the throat and raced out an open door. I would have yelled good riddance, but I knew he would be back.

The movers worked all morning unloading the van, while Rick looked suspiciously at the number of boxes labeled *attic*. Later in the day, he suggested I take a break and drive to Home Depot to pick up a few things we needed. I was happy to leave him in charge of the house and escaped before he changed his mind.

I arrived at Home Depot and searched for the items on Rick's list but came up empty-handed. I was on my way to the Customer Service counter when I saw an employee coming down the aisle.

"Excuse me, sir. Could you . . ."

Before I finished speaking, he barked, "Let me tell you how we do things here. I'm helping someone else. When I finish helping them, I'll help you. OK? You got that?"

"Yes," I replied.

He walked past me, and I fled out the front door. By the time I reached the car, I was crying. What had I done wrong? I had made a simple request for assistance. Rick would have to make do with what he had. I was too upset to go inside again.

To ease my despair, I stopped at the Dunkin' Donuts in Bryn Mawr and picked up some muffins and coffee to take home. An employee handed me my order, and I turned to leave. Just as I walked out, I remembered our silverware was still packed, so I went back inside and asked for some utensils and napkins.

"Who waited on you?" mumbled the woman at the counter.

"The person by the coffee machine."

"Then he's who ya gotta ask," she said as she began rolling out dough.

I was speechless. Why couldn't she give me what I needed? If my arms were longer, I would have reached over the counter and gotten everything for myself. What was the point of making the man who waited on me, who was now busy filling the coffee machine, interrupt his work to hand me a few spoons and napkins?

I drove home confused and frustrated and found Rick in the kitchen trying to reassemble our dining room table. I set the bag from Dunkin' Donuts on the counter, put my arms around his waist and laid my head against his chest.

"What's wrong?" he asked.

"Everything. The rules are different here, and I don't know them. I don't even know anyone to ask. What am I going to do?"

"Let's take a break and have a glass of wine. There's someone I want you to meet."

That someone was Kathy Engebretson. She was our new neighbor, and she quickly became my friend. Rick and Kathy worked together at Penn, and he often mentioned her. When he learned she lived around the corner from our new home, he decided to wait until after our move to surprise me with the news.

"Nancy!" she said as she opened the front door holding a precious little girl. "I've been dying to meet you. This is Emma. She just woke up. Most babies are happy after a nap, but not Emma. She always wakes up mad."

I liked everything about Kathy: her warmth, her enthusiasm and her candor. She grew up in the Midwest and had that marvelous matter-of-fact, no-nonsense attitude that seems to come naturally to Midwesterners. She was something of a legend in Philadelphia. In 1992, Mayor Ed Rendell recruited her from Lehman Brothers in New York to help lead the city back to financial stability. When she became city treasurer, Philly faced a one hundred fifty-three million dollar budget deficit; its bond rating had slipped to junk status, and lenders withdrew their support. During her tenure, she not only stabilized the city's fiscal structure but also secured three billion dollars in funding. It was one of the most remarkable turnarounds in urban history.

After leaving her job as City Treasurer, Kathy worked with the World Bank to develop a pooled loan program for historically black colleges and universities. In her spare time, she earned her Ph.D. at the Wharton School of Business at Penn. Although she had never married, she dreamed of being a mother, and after learning of the horrific conditions in many of the orphanages in China, she applied to adopt a baby girl. When we met, she had recently returned to Philadelphia to assume the role of Penn's Vice-President for Finance.

Kathy was quick to extend her friendship, and I was eager to reciprocate. We took Emma on walks through the neighborhood, met for pizza and often shared late night dinners. When she needed a baby sitter, all she had to do was ask.

Kathy was the most accomplished and sophisticated woman I had ever known. I grew in many ways from our relationship, but I wondered what she saw in me. I certainly hadn't achieved much. My entire resume could fit on the back of a paper napkin. I commented on this one day as we were walking with Emma, and Kathy stopped and looked at me with a puzzled expression.

"Are you serious? You are a sincere, caring person, and I treasure your friendship. Don't confuse self-worth with achievements. They are not nearly as important as character. Some of the worst human beings I know are some of the most accomplished."

Having a person I admired and respected hold me in high regard was an awakening of sorts. Adjusting to life in a mega-city like Philadelphia was harder than I had imagined, and since moving there, my self-confidence had waned. I was afraid of trying because I was terrified of failure. Kathy valued me as a person, and she reminded me to value myself.

I was unloading groceries one afternoon when she knocked on the back door.

"Do you have time to talk?" she asked.

"Of course, come on in. I'll make us some tea after I get these things put away."

Kathy sat down at the kitchen table. She was quiet, and I noticed her usual bright smile was missing. Something was troubling her, but I didn't pry.

"I've accepted a job with a new internet start-up venture, BET.com. One of its goals is to attract more African Americans to the internet. Microsoft is one of their partners," she said.

"Awesome! When do you begin?"

"That's the hard part. They want me there as soon as possible, but it means moving to D.C. I like Washington, but I hate uprooting Emma and putting her through so much change."

"Are you certain this is something you want to do?"

"It's not an option," she snapped.

Her brusqueness puzzled me. I wondered if her job at Penn had anything to do with her decision. We rarely talked about her work, but when we did, I sensed she wasn't entirely happy.

"Emma will be fine. As long as the two of you are together, everything will be all right."

Kathy was not a demonstrative person, so I was surprised when she hugged me before leaving. Within a month, the windows in her house were dark, and she and Emma were gone. Over the course of the next year or so, we had little contact. The long hours required to ensure the success of BET.com and helping Emma assimilate into her new surroundings left her with little time for anything else. I missed my friend and our frank discussions and spontaneous walks through the neighborhood.

It was a dreary, rainy day, and the small windows and low ceiling in our den made it feel like a tomb. The silence I relished when we moved to Bryn Mawr was now driving me crazy. I had exhausted my interest in all things domestic and couldn't have cared less if the walls in our living room were painted "French Vanilla" or "Concord Yellow." It was time to get a job.

I perused Penn's website daily in hopes of discovering a new niche. After fifteen years of teaching, I was ready for a different challenge. There were plenty of opportunities at Penn, but none of them appealed to me. For example, there was a position in the School of Veterinary Medicine. I gave it serious consideration. I like animals, sort of, but not that much. There was also an opening in Development and Alumni Relations, but I was told it involved sixty percent travel. After two years of living apart, I wasn't about to take a position requiring me to be away from Rick three or four nights a week.

I was sitting at my computer ready to call it quits on another unsuccessful day of job hunting when a new posting appeared. The Office of Undergraduate Admissions was recruiting an Assistant Director for On-Campus Programs. Responsibilities included oversight of the university's campus tour guides and student ambassadors, coordinating Penn Preview Days and supervising student workers. With the exception of the student workers, all the programs relied on volunteers. These students devoted time each week to sharing their knowledge and love of Penn with prospective applicants and their parents.

I had found my niche. This job would satisfy my desire to explore a new career yet still allow me to interact with students. The next morning, I updated my resume and sent it to Dean Lee Stetson, Office of Undergraduate Admissions, The University of Pennsylvania. When I shared the news with Rick, he was less than enthusiastic.

"I wish we'd talked before you applied. Have you considered whether this is fair to Kathryn?"

"What are you talking about? What does this have to do with Kathryn?"

"It has a lot to do with her. She already has one parent on campus. Undergraduate Admissions is in College Hall. If you get this job, your office will be right in the center of campus, and she'll be tempted to stop by every time she needs help. I just don't want Penn to become an extension of high school. This should be a time when she learns to stand on her own two feet."

I sulked but knew Rick was right. I should have considered the impact this could have on Kathryn. Before going to bed, I made a mental note to give her a call the next day.

The phone rang a few hours later and startled me. I have always had an intense fear of late night calls, so I braced myself for the worst before picking up the receiver.

"Hello?"

"Hey, Mom! What are you guys up to?"

"Kathryn?"

"Yes?"

"What's wrong? Why are you calling so late?"

"I thought it was early and you'd still be up. I just called to say hello before we go out."

"Go out? What do you mean, 'go out'? It's late, and you're in West Philadelphia. Where are you going?"

"We're going to Center City."

"Center City! Are you crazy? It's eleven o'clock at night. Don't you realize how dangerous the city can be at this hour? What are you planning to do?"

"We're going to a club."

"You're not twenty-one. How are you going to get in a club?"

I knew what her answer would be before she even said it.

"I have a fake I.D."

"Oh, a fake I.D. Tell me something. Do you also have a *get out of jail free* card? I hope so because you're going to need it. The moment you flash that I.D., you have committed a crime. Don't you realize the clubs in Center City are full of under-cover cops watching for underage drinkers?"

"Mom, you don't have to worry. Nothing's going to happen."

"Kathryn, no one who ever stood in front of a judge thought something was going to happen."

I hung up, stared at the ceiling and waited for the sun to rise. I reasoned if no one phoned us before morning, she was probably safe. When the first glimpse of light hit our windows, I closed my eyes and went to sleep.

Rick, of course, slept through the entire episode. His face turned red the next morning when I told him about Kathryn's call, and he left the house before finishing his coffee. Kathryn later informed me he called her on his way to work and told her I was awake all night worrying. He gave her explicit instructions that in the future she was to keep her plans to herself. He also reminded her she was an adult and he expected her to use sound judgment. He said if she had a fake ID and didn't destroy it before noon; he would move her out of the Quad and into our home in Bryn Mawr. His threats must have worked, because she never phoned us that late again, nor did she ever mention a fake ID.

The transition to parenting a college student was difficult. As Rick reminded me, it would be easy to let our close proximity to Kathryn become more of a hindrance than a help. Then again, after learning about her escapades into Center City, I thought the center of campus might be exactly where I belonged. I decided to call Undergraduate Admissions and inquire about my resume.

I was smiling the next day when I hung up the phone. Dean Stetson wanted to meet with me on Friday to discuss the position in On-Campus Programs. I had a lot to learn before then, but if I could convince the Dean to hire me, I knew I would be perfect for the job.

On Friday, I arrived at the Office of Undergraduate Admissions and met the Dean's assistant, Heather Heard. Heather was an attractive, thirty-something blonde with a beautiful smile.

"The Dean is on a conference call, but he'll be with you in just a few minutes. If you wait here, someone will let you know when he's available."

I took a seat and Heather disappeared down the hallway. I was looking forward to meeting Dean Stetson. There are few areas within a university more scrutinized or more controversial than undergraduate admissions. The fact that Dean Stetson had managed to hold onto his job at Penn for almost thirty years was remarkable. Since becoming Dean, applications had risen, diversity had improved and the number of foreign students had increased. He was considered one of the most influential figures in Ivy League admissions.

While I waited for my interview, I reviewed my talking points. When I finished, I browsed through a magazine. After that, I memorized the names of Penn's past presidents engraved on a nearby plaque. I checked the time and realized it was after five o'clock. I wondered how much longer I would have to wait. I closed my eyes and rested my head against the back of the chair. After a while, I looked at my watch again. Another thirty minutes had passed, and still no sign of the Dean. I walked through the office trying to locate Heather, but most of the lights were off, and the desks were empty. I went back and sat down again. The next time I checked my watch, it was six o'clock.

The situation was becoming awkward. Should I wait for the cleaning crew to kick me out or knock on the Dean's door and remind him I was waiting? I decided on the latter course. I was gathering my belongings just as the door opened and a young man gestured for me to enter. I approached the doorway tentatively and stepped inside.

The lighting in the Dean's office was dim, and it took a moment for my eyes to adjust. When they did, I noticed a man seated on the couch across the room. He was wearing a black suit, black shirt and purple tie. I saw his picture on Penn's website and knew he was Dean Stetson.

The young man who opened the door smiled and extended his hand.

"Nancy, I'm Eric Kaplan, Associate Dean of Admissions. It's a pleasure to meet you."

I liked Eric from the moment we met. The daily pressures of Ivy League admissions hadn't robbed him of his boyish smile or warm, relaxed demeanor. After we shook hands, an awkward pause ensued while we both waited for the Dean to speak. When it became apparent he didn't intend to introduce himself, Eric jumped in and rescued the situation.

"Nancy, this is Lee Stetson, Dean of Admissions."

The Dean rose and said, "Thank you for meeting with us, Nancy. I understand you're interested in On-Campus Programs."

Although no one invited me to sit, I did so anyway.

"Yes, I read about the position and . . ."

"Nancy, I want you to know I have high regard for Rick. He is doing a terrific job at Penn. He gets things done, and he's accomplished a lot since he came. We were fortunate to recruit him from Vanderbilt. I'm sure leaving Nashville was a hard decision."

"Yes, but . . ."

"I hope Rick plans to be here a long time because there's still plenty to do."

"I'm sure he . . ."

"About the job, Nancy. I expect loyalty, commitment and discretion from my team. You will be interacting with some very distinguished people, and there is no room for error. This office is the face of the university."

"I understand, and . . ."

"I'm sure you'll be an excellent addition to our staff. I'll leave it to Eric to work out the details."

With that said, Dean Stetson picked up a file and began working. The interview lasted less than ten minutes, and I hadn't asked or answered a single question. The Dean knew nothing about me, and I knew next to nothing about the job.

"Nancy, if you'll follow me, I'll show you out. The building is probably locked by now," Eric said.

I wanted to thank the Dean for the opportunity he was giving me, but he was engrossed in his reading. I turned and followed Eric out of the office and down the hall.

"Eric, do you mind if I ask you something?"

"Not at all."

"Was that a typical Lee Stetson interview?"

"Nancy, there's nothing typical about Lee Stetson."

He smiled, took a key out of his pocket and unlocked the door of College Hall.

"I'll give you a call in the next couple of days to discuss your new role. Welcome to Penn."

Occasionally, there are experiences for which we think we are prepared, but in reality, there is no possible way we could be. The first day I entered the world of Ivy League admissions, I was energized, optimistic and more than a little green. When I left Penn seven years later, my idealism had faded, and I wasn't the least bit naïve.

I arrived home from work one afternoon and heard the phone ringing. I fumbled with the key and then rushed across the room to catch the call. It was Kathy and she sounded excited.

"I'm in Philadelphia with Emma, and we have some good news. We're moving back to Bryn Mawr! I just made an offer on a house only five minutes from you."

The William Penn Foundation, a prominent philanthropic organization in Philadelphia, asked Kathy to become its next president, and she accepted. I was thrilled she and Emma were returning to Philadelphia, and we made plans to meet later that night at our favorite pizza place.

Emma waved when I entered the restaurant. She was laughing as she bounced up and down on the cushioned seat in the booth where she and Kathy sat. I waved back and crossed the room. After giving Emma a quick hug, I turned to Kathy. Her appearance startled me. It was obvious she had lost a lot of weight, but there was more, something else. It was her hair. The style she was wearing made it look much thicker, and a few minutes later, I realized it wasn't a new style at all. Kathy was wearing a wig. Because of Emma's presence, I was reluctant to mention anything about the change in her appearance. We ate dinner, laughed and caught up on our lives, but as we said goodbye, I couldn't shake the feeling that something was wrong.

Kathy loved working for the foundation. She said giving money away was the best job anyone could ever have. It was wonderful to have her and Emma nearby, but getting together wasn't easy. We made plans, but she'd often bow out at the last minute. She sounded tired, but I attributed it to the demands of a new position. Sadly, I was wrong.

Rick came home late one night and barely spoke at dinner. It was often difficult for him to let go of work, so I wasn't concerned. After we ate, I did the dishes while he caught up on the news. After putting the last dish away, I joined him in the living room. He motioned for me to sit next to him.

"There's something I need to tell you."

It was evident from the serious look on his face that something was terribly wrong and I didn't want to hear it.

"Kathy announced today that she'll be leaving her job at the end of the month."

"Why would she do that? She loves her work."

"Apparently, she was diagnosed with breast cancer while she was living in DC. She's been in remission for over a year, but the cancer has come back and spread to other parts of her body. Her doctors told her it's inoperable."

It took some time for Rick's words to sink in, but when they did, all the pieces fell into place - the weight loss, the wig, Kathy's chronic fatigue, and our broken dates. Cancer explained everything except why she didn't tell me. I could have helped her. Why had she shut me out? When I spoke with Kathy, her answer was simple and honest.

"There's so little you have control over when something like this happens. I wanted my time with Emma to be as normal as possible, so I decided not to tell anyone I was sick until it became absolutely necessary."

Kathy had three to six months to live, and she wanted to spend as much time as possible with Emma. I planned my visits for times when Emma was at school and always phoned before going to her house.

"Kathy, if you're not up to having company, just tell me, and I won't come," I said on the phone one night.

"No. I want you to come. Please come."

I could tell from her voice how difficult it was for her to speak, so we only talked a few minutes.

"I love you, Kathy. I'll see you Tuesday."

"I love you, too."

That was Friday. On Monday, Kathy died. She was the first friend I lost to cancer and the person who taught me how to say goodbye forever.

Emma moved to the Midwest to live with Kathy's sister, and I never saw her again. The William Penn Foundation established a scholarship in Kathy's memory that provides assistance with education expenses for women in challenging circumstances. Governor Ed Rendell told the *Philadelphia Inquirer*, "Kathy Engebretson had it all. She was bright, talented, charming and nice. No matter what she did, she did well, with tremendous class and grace."

The world and all of us who loved her were short-changed by Kathy's passing. She possessed greatness and limitless compassion. At age forty-eight, her achievements were already manifold. Kathy was proud of the work she did, but she never boasted. As I watched her relinquish her life, I didn't witness a bitter, resentful person. She died at peace with herself. She believed what she told me the day we went for a walk: Don't confuse self-worth with achievements. Value people for who they are, not what they are. Accepting myself for who I am, and not what I am, is the legacy Kathy left me. I thought I understood the depth of its importance, but I didn't . . . not for several years.

NURTURING INSANITY

24

I frantically searched through the top drawer of my desk for the OxyContin prescribed months ago for an abscessed tooth. The last time I looked, there were at least two pills in the bottle.

"Nancy, how many students from Long Island were admitted to Penn last year?" Peter yelled from the phone room.

"Twenty-four," I shouted.

Calls were coming into the admissions office faster than we could answer them. Early decision letters were being released that week, and applicants were growing anxious for their results.

"Nancy, when are Penn Preview Days?" Angela called.

"April 12 – 16."

The answers to all their questions were posted on the inside covers of the notebooks placed by each phone, yet my student workers would rather yell their questions than take the time to look up an answer.

Maybe the pills were in the back of my file cabinet. They had to be here somewhere.

"Nancy, can I leave early today to study for my econ exam?" Tyler shouted.

"That's the same excuse you gave on Monday when you left early. No one has two econ exams in one week. The answer is no. If you hadn't lied, it would have been yes."

If I could just find those pills, my headache would be gone in no time. I dug through another drawer and finally found the bottle. My memory was correct; inside were two tiny white tablets. I grabbed a bottle of water and popped one in my mouth.

The seven students working in our phone room were an unruly bunch with a knack for playing jokes and showing up late. Everything they did involved negotiation. For instance, on Fridays, if they showed up for work on time, I allowed them to use fake accents when answering calls. Their dialects were quite realistic, and they managed to pull their deception off without a single glitch. Penn's diversity was never greater than on Fridays when voices from Great Britain, Italy, Ireland, Germany and more could be heard echoing through our office.

When I wasn't monitoring phone room antics, I was busy recruiting and training students to serve as campus tour guides or ambassadors. Successful applicants were out-going, articulate, and attractive. The importance of the latter attribute was brought to my attention through a series of communications designed to obscure the original source—though there was little doubt it came from the top. Each semester, new tour guides and ambassadors went through rigorous training designed to indoctrinate them in all things Penn. In addition, they received coaching on diplomacy, poise and, due to a regrettable incident occurring on my watch, time management.

Tours of Penn are designed to take approximately one hour, and campus guides are expected to honor this timeframe. I was busy in my office late one afternoon when I received a call from Ryan, one of the renegades from the phone room.

"You'll never guess who I just passed on Locust Walk."

"I don't have time for games. Either tell me or hang up."

"It was the princess."

The princess was Allison Berkston, a sophomore from Long Island. She was a sweet girl, but clueless. The phone room gang selected her nickname due to her questionable presence at Penn and badgered me relentlessly to access her file so they could determine why she was admitted.

This was Allison's first semester as a campus tour guide. She was here at the request of the Dean, so I tried to make the best of it. Nevertheless, I could tell from the glee in Ryan's voice that something was going on and I probably wouldn't like it.

"You called just to tell me you passed Allison on Locust Walk?"

"No, I called to tell you I passed her *and* her tour group."

"What are you talking about? She left here at one o'clock just like you."

"I know, but *my* tour ended two hours ago."

"What time is it?"

"Four-thirty."

"Are you telling me she's held those people hostage for three hours?"

"That's exactly what I'm telling you."

I couldn't believe what I was hearing. Three hours of mind numbing commentary by Allison was enough to drive a person insane.

"If you take charge of her group, and get them back here in the next fifteen minutes, I won't ask you to lead a tour for the rest of the month."

"Six weeks, or the answer is no."

"Six weeks, and you swear never to mention this to anyone."

"Agreed."

"Good. Now go rescue those poor people, and tell Allison I need to see her right now."

I went in my office, shut the door and screamed.

"Nancy, are you all right?" someone shouted from the phone room.

"I'm okay. I accidentally stapled my thumb."

"Well, try to keep it down. The game's on."

The game's on? What game? I fumbled for the bottle of OxyContin and took the other pill.

My job could be summed up in one word - unpredictable. The number of daily visitors to our office could vary from five to five hundred. On any given day, with no prior notice, I might need as few as two tour guides or as many as twenty. Regardless, I was expected to be prepared.

I solved my dilemma by requiring all the student workers to train as tour guides. By doing so, I was assured of having sufficient help to manage any situation. I thought my idea was brilliant but not the gang in the phone room. They hated me for adding this new responsibility to their otherwise unexacting portfolio of work. Whenever forced to leave their comfortable seats, they gave me the evil eye. I decided a bribe was in order and placed a candy dish by each phone. It's amazing how much forgiveness you can buy with a bag of Hershey Kisses.

Unlike some universities, Penn made the decision years ago not to wall itself off from the surrounding community. I believe it was the right thing to do, but an open campus in the center of a large city generates a number of unique challenges. For example, adding to the already erratic atmosphere of our office was the fact that a rather loosely run mental health facility stood only a few blocks away. Patients somehow regularly managed, without much difficulty, to escape their confinement and find their way to Penn Admissions.

One elderly patient repeatedly showed up to our office, usually within minutes of a scheduled information session, insisting she was sent by God to remove all her clothes. Between the time she arrived and the time authorities could respond, it was a struggle to keep her dressed. I am not sure what went through the minds of our prospective students and their parents as they watched this fiasco unfold, but I would be surprised if it were positive. The first time I witnessed it, I was appalled, but after a while, it became just another hiccup in the day.

As the official welcome center for prospective students, the doors of the admissions office are rarely closed. I was alone in our central reception area one afternoon when a young man in his mid-twenties entered. The moment I saw him, I knew something was wrong. His eyes were glazed, and he looked as if he hadn't bathed in a month.

He stumbled to the counter and in slurred speech mumbled, "I'm going to shoot everybody at Villanova."

I didn't know if he was carrying a gun, but he seemed too far gone to be a threat.

"I'm sorry, but this isn't Villanova. This is Penn. Villanova is about fifteen miles west. Still, as long as you're here, why don't you take a tour of campus?"

His dazed look told me he had no idea what I meant.

"Take this map, and turn right when you go out the door. In front of this building, you will find a statue of Benjamin Franklin. Stand next to the statue and a student will be there soon to show you around campus."

He took the map and exited our office. I phoned the Penn police, and within minutes, they had him surrounded. As they hauled him away, I noticed he was still clutching the map I had given him. Was it possible he thought he was on the tour?

Later in the day, while leading a group of visitors through campus, one of our tour guides suffered a slight concussion. She was standing in front of the Wharton School of Business when a hefty squirrel fell from the canopy of trees above her and knocked her down. I was called to the scene and arrived just as the poor girl was being carried away.

"Are we still going to get our tour?" asked a disgruntled member of her abandoned group.

I smiled politely and said, "Yes, indeed. College Hall is just a two-minute walk. In front of the building, you will find a statue of Benjamin Franklin. If you wait next to the statue, a tour guide will meet you to show you around campus."

I've often wondered how long they waited.

THE IVY MYSTIQUE

25

A certain mystique existed regarding admission to Penn. On the surface, everything appeared impartial, but decisions often left families baffled and suspicious of the process. I once thought hard work and commitment were the keys to being a successful applicant, but my naiveté vanished after joining the Office of Undergraduate Admissions. A different set of criteria existed behind the scenes . . . conditions beyond the control of the applicant. While it's true every application to Penn is read at least once, the speed with which it is read and marked *Denied* can be staggering. With over thirty-one thousand applicants for only twenty-four hundred spots in the freshman class, the ability to perform a critical evaluation of each application doesn't exist.

"Our goal is not to admit a particular type of student but to assemble a diverse class of talented scholars from around the world."

This tenet was at the core of all policies related to admissions at Penn. The Dean's stance was well known to the public, and I agreed with the principle behind his philosophy. However, principles are meaningless if they are compromised, and policies are worthless unless practiced.

As for being denied admission, all things being equal, it was generally due to one of two things: either the applicant had no advocate (high school counselors make great advocates because admission officers like to keep them happy; happy counselors equal more applicants) or he or she satisfied no particular need at the university. Rest assured the Penn Band's request for a new bassoon player will trump the young woman who did well in five advanced placement courses. Void of an advocate or the ability to satisfy a need at the university, an application was generally dead before a second read.

Of course, the numbers game also came into play. Heaven help any applicant from Pennsylvania, New York, New Jersey or California – the states with Penn's highest number of applicants.

How do you tell a boy from New Jersey who runs a food pantry for the poor, spent two summers in Mexico building houses for the homeless, works fourteen hours a week bagging groceries and is president of his class - all while maintaining a 3.9 GPA - that his chance of being admitted is slim because, darn it, there are just too many applicants from his home state.

On the other hand, if he were willing to move to North Dakota, it's a different story. Universities in the northeast are begging for applicants from North Dakota. The chance of a *B* student from North Dakota being admitted into one of the Ivies is twice as high as an *A* student from New Jersey. I wouldn't be surprised if more students didn't start spending their senior year in Bismarck.

"There's a lot wrong in college admissions," a friend and former admissions officer at Penn told me. "It's a field where you don't have to be extremely bright or even sincere to be successful. With little or no training, admissions officers are given the power to play God and socially engineer a college class."

When I arrived at Penn, I was caught off-guard by the degree of importance placed on an Ivy League education. High school juniors and seniors intent on making good impressions showed up in our office dressed like models from a Ralph Lauren showroom. Gifts of candy, fruit, and cookies arrived daily, and admission officers, most of whom acknowledge they would never have been accepted to Penn themselves, were treated with a degree of respect typically reserved for royalty.

Where I came from, it was enough to get in *any* college. Natives of the Northeast, however, saw things a bit differently . . . especially parents.

I remember the day I met the Harvey family. It was a quarter after two, and they were running late. This wasn't unusual. The time required to park and walk to the Admissions Office takes much longer than expected and usually invokes frustration.

When the door of the Admissions Office eventually opened, three people drenched by the day's heavy rain and gusting wind stumbled inside. Their faces were red, and they were out of breath.

"Shit," said the man whom I presumed to be Mr. Harvey. "It's pouring, and your parking garage is at least a twenty- minute walk from here."

I restrained myself from reminding him it wasn't *my* parking garage.

"Welcome to Penn," I said cheerfully.

I knew my jubilant greeting would further irritate Mr. Harvey, but he was so unpleasant. Erica Harvey, a freshman at the University of Virginia (UVA), had phoned the prior week and asked to meet with a representative of our office to discuss transferring to Penn. After seating the Harveys in our conference room, I congratulated Erica on her acceptance to UVA.

"It's quite an accomplishment. UVA is an outstanding university with a stellar reputation."

"I told her it was a good school," Mr. Harvey grumbled to no one in particular.

I studied Erica's face and tried to imagine what was running through her mind.

"Are you enjoying your first semester, Erica?"

"She likes it just fine, but it's not Penn, and she has her heart set on going to Penn," said Mrs. Harvey.

I glanced at Erica, who looked down at the floor. I didn't blame her.

"What attracts you to Penn, Erica?"

"Erica has loved Penn since our first visit," Mrs. Harvey said. "She applied early decision but was wait-listed. We're hoping she will be more successful when she applies as a transfer student. We thought you might give us some advice on how to help her. I know we're only midway through the first semester, but she is doing extremely well. I'm sure she will end up with at least a 3.5 GPA."

Mrs. Harvey seemed sure of everything, but I wondered about Erica. Although I continued to address my questions directly to her; this did nothing to deter her mother.

"A lot of emphasis is placed on the GPA of transfer students, and it sounds like you're off to a great start. I've put together some materials I think might be helpful if you decide to apply. We also accept second year transfer students, so please don't be hasty in making your decision."

"Erica's going to apply. She loves Penn," Mrs. Harvey said.

"What do you like most about Penn, Erica?"

Poor Erica struggled to respond in a manner worthy of a successful transfer applicant.

"I guess I like everything about it."

"Is there something you don't like about UVA?"

Erica was at a loss for words. Apparently, Mrs. Harvey's coaching failed to address every possibility.

"Well, no matter. It's been a pleasure to meet you and your family. I hope you'll continue to do well and enjoy your first year of college."

I showed the Harvey family to the door. The rain was coming down in sheets, and it was beginning to thunder. I stood at the window watching them dash to the parking garage and made a mental note to check in a few months on whether Erica applied to Penn. I was almost certain she would. Mrs. Harvey would make sure of it. I witnessed scenarios similar to Erica's play out dozens of times, but I never became immune to how it dishonored students who deserved so much better.

Do you want what's best for your child, or do you just want the best? It was a question I often had to squelch when meeting with parents. It's also a question I learned to ask myself. There should be a sign above the door of the Office of Undergraduate Admissions with words similar to those my friend Kathy shared: *Don't confuse your son or daughter's self-worth with achievements. They aren't nearly as important as character.*

Penn forced me to confront my life-long battle with poor self-esteem. The culture and people I encountered were sophisticated and formidable. In order to be successful in my role, I needed to engage at their level – there was never a question they would stoop to mine. It was a challenge but also an opportunity. As time passed, I learned to hold my own in groups that once intimidated me. My confidence soared and with it, my happiness.

The environment in Penn Admissions was relaxed and friendly and made up for the long days and occasional weekends we had to work. However, that situation could change quickly if the right person walked in.

"The Dean is on his way here."

I looked up just in time to see Ryan dash pass my door.

"Wait a minute! Come back! How do you know?"

"Shannon called."

Like all my student workers, Ryan knew exactly what to do if the Dean made one of his infrequent visits to campus. I picked up the phone and dialed the receptionist in International Admissions.

"The Dean is on his way here," I said.

I ducked into the phone room where, of course, I found my under-ambitious student workers breaking every rule I had ever made. Their shirts were hanging out, their feet were bare, two of them were popping gum while talking to callers and one was engrossed in a personal conversation and had her phone set on *busy*.

"Listen up! The Dean is on his way here."

Everything came to a screeching halt. Clothes were adjusted, gum went in the trash, shoes reappeared and every phone was promptly answered. I checked the reception area and found two student ambassadors straightening bookshelves and collecting discarded newspapers. God bless them. When I needed those kids, they always came through.

The Dean's unique persona created a strange environment in the office. Simply stated, he was unreadable. His unpredictable nature kept all of us on our toes and quaking in our shoes. He was famous for leaving loud, angry phone messages expressing displeasure over insignificant matters. He also had a peculiar way of using others to relay his directives. It wasn't unusual to have co-workers drop hints that, in the future, the Dean might like for this or that to be done another way. To be fair, he could also be extremely complimentary and appreciative. Unfortunately, no one trusted his better side.

MINOR CONFLICTS 26

Although life in the Admissions Office had its difficulties, Kathryn couldn't have been happier at Penn. Within weeks of arriving on campus, she joined a co-ed jazz and pop *a cappella* group called *Counterparts*. The musical director of the group was a senior named John Stephens. The first time I saw John perform, his incredible voice and musical arrangements blew me away. There was never an empty seat when Counterparts performed.

In addition to volunteer performances throughout the year, Counterparts also presented fall and spring concerts. The second semester of Kathryn's freshman year, she was given a solo in the spring show. It seemed an opportune time for a visit from my mother, so we arranged for her to travel to Philadelphia.

The site of the performance was Penn's stunning, newly renovated Irvine Auditorium. The night of the show, we drove into the city early to secure prime seats. As the lights dimmed and the group took the stage, they were met with thunderous applause. The first act was spectacular. As usual, John's powerful voice mesmerized the audience.

After a short intermission, Counterparts returned to the stage to even louder, more enthusiastic applause. The house lights dimmed, and Kathryn stepped forward into a solitary spotlight. The rest of the ensemble stood behind her and began their background harmonies. I couldn't have been happier for her or for the opportunity to have my mother share this experience with me. As I settled into my seat and prepared to enjoy Kathryn's big moment, I felt tremendous pride and more than a little smug. That's when it happened. That was the moment my daughter opened her mouth and belted out the words,

"I don't want anybody else. When I think about you, I touch myself."

What did she just say? She didn't say what I thought she said – did she? I must have misunderstood the lyrics, but why was she standing on stage with throaty moans escaping from her mouth? I listened carefully as the words were repeated. It was true. My daughter was standing on stage, in front of my mother, singing about masturbating. Where was the girl who throughout high school charmed church congregations everywhere with her rendition of *He Never Failed Me Yet*? Out of the corner of my eye, I saw Rick shake his head in a gesture of defeat.

The song ended and the audience, all except the three people with prime seats who appeared to be suffering from post-traumatic shock, rose to its feet in a standing ovation. I turned to my mother and was about to attempt a plausible explanation when she leaned over and said,

"Kathryn's always had such a lovely voice."

Her support should not have surprised me. After all, she was my mother, and she had suffered through far more shocking behavior than what I just witnessed.

We quickly headed for the door. I was not up to confronting Kathryn, but that didn't deter her persistence. She rushed up the aisle to solicit our feedback. I suspected she knew what mine would be but hoped her grandmother's presence might cushion my response.

"So, what did you think?"

"You sang well."

"Why do you look angry?"

"I'm not angry."

"Yes, you are. You didn't like the song, did you?"

"Don't be presumptuous."

"I'm not. I can tell you didn't like it, so why won't you be honest?"

"I was trying not to spoil your evening, but if you insist on talking about this, then we will. You're right. I didn't like the song. It's about masturbating. How would you like to sit in the audience and listen to *me* sing about it? Why didn't you warn me before you let me invite your grandmother?"

"Mom, do you seriously think Grandmother understands what that song is about?"

"Kathryn, never underestimate my mother. She may be getting on in years, but she's not stupid."

Kathryn turned and left in a huff. I was weary and went in search of my mother. I found her standing across the room with Rick. He was attempting to engage her in a conversation about the arts in order to distract her, but he had forgotten my mother is not easily duped. As she took my arm and we headed out the door, she whispered, "Don't worry. It could be a lot worse."

I just smiled. We both knew she was thinking of me.

At the end of each year, Counterparts creates a CD of their most popular songs. John was adamant Kathryn's performance of *I Touch Myself* be included, and I was determined it would not be. I knew Kathryn was wrestling with both demands, and I was relieved when she stopped by my office to announce she wouldn't be performing the song.

"You've made the right decision, Kathryn."

"I don't know if I have or not, but it's what you want."

As she turned and walked out the door, instead of feeling triumphant, I had an odd feeling I had made a serious mistake.

Later in the afternoon, Kathryn forwarded me the response she had received from John after informing him of her decision. I read each line and wondered how someone only twenty-one years old could be so astute.

"Kathryn, if this is your final decision, I'll accept it, but I want you to know how disappointed I am your song won't be on the CD. I respect your desire to do what your parents want, but what you want is also important. This is your freshman year, and your parents are no doubt struggling with your independence. Sometimes parents have a hard time acknowledging their child isn't a child any longer. It took my parents a while to stop thinking of me as little Johnny. They weren't accustomed to hearing me sing about adult things, but I am an adult. I hope you will change your mind. The song is powerful, and I arranged it just for you. It would be a shame to exclude it from this year's CD."

When I finished reading John's email, I picked up the phone and called Kathryn. She answered on the first ring.

"Kathryn, knowing the right thing to do in every circumstance is hard. Even parents have trouble figuring it out. I was wrong to say you couldn't sing on the CD. This is your decision to make and your responsibility. Making decisions and taking responsibility for them isn't easy, but it's what turns a child into an adult. If you decide to sing on the CD, I'll accept it. It's your life, and I'll try to stop living it for you"

"Mom?"

"Yes?"

"I'm going to record the song."

"I know."

I hung up the phone and gave my mother a call.

A few months later, John Stephens graduated from Penn, and he continued to pursue his musical interests. A few years later, his debut album, *Get Lifted*, went platinum, and to date, he has won nine Grammy Awards, a Golden Globe and an Oscar. His single release *All of Me* hit number one on Billboard's Hot 100 chart. His success was hard earned and much deserved. Kudos to you, John – best known today as John Legend – for many things.

MAJOR ASSAULTS

27

How you feel about your life can alter your perspective of time. At least, that is how the theory goes. Maybe it explains why my years in Philadelphia seemed to go by in such a rapid, brilliant blur. They were transformative years full of fresh experiences and new knowledge. My first exposure to fine art, music, the ballet and opera occurred during those years. It was a time when I changed and grew in more ways than I can count, but nothing in life remains static. Times change, people change and circumstances alter. I was familiar with the scenario.

The dawn of Kathryn's senior year reminded me another door would soon close. Decisions had to be made and plans put in place. It was a year that threatened to overwhelm me. However, that was before the worst day imaginable happened. After that day, my perspective on almost everything changed, and I reexamined my priorities.

It began as an ordinary morning. I left my office and headed for the reception area to meet with some freshmen who were hoping for jobs in our phone room. I was not in a particularly good mood. I hated the beginning of fall semester because it meant filling positions vacated by my seasoned student workers who graduated the previous spring. Training new students was rewarding but time consuming, and time was in short supply.

As I entered the room, our receptionist looked up from her computer. Her mouth was hanging open, and her eyes were as big as saucers.

"Shannon, are you all right? What's the matter?"

"A plane just hit the World Trade Center."

"Are they calling it a terrorist attack?"

Shannon slowly nodded yes. I raced to our media room and found a handful of my colleagues gathered in front of the television. CNN was broadcasting scenes from New York.

"What's happening? What's going on?"

"A second plane crashed into another tower, and they just announced other planes are unaccounted for."

As news of the disaster spread, Penn went on high alert. Classes were canceled, and the university closed. Before leaving campus, Rick and I tried to convince Kathryn to come to Bryn Mawr, but she insisted on remaining with her friends. We honored her request and drove home in silence while listening to the news. It would be one of the longest nights of my life and one of the saddest days in history. It was September 11, 2001.

The next day a new normal rose from the ashes and replaced my once familiar routine. Waking up became synonymous with turning on the news and praying for an uneventful day. I called my family and friends more often, fell asleep each night holding Rick's hand and never let a day go by without emailing Kathryn to say, "I love you."

The attack on 9/11 sent the U.S. economy tumbling. Enrollment in graduate schools soared as students sought refuge from a slim job market. Kathryn had decided to pursue a legal career and requested applications from a dozen law schools. The number of applicants to law schools rose by over forty percent that year. Kathryn told us she would attend the best school to which she was accepted. That school turned out to be Vanderbilt University Law School. Kathryn would soon be on her way back to Nashville.

9/11 affected everyone, and Kathryn was no exception. She evaluated her remaining time at Penn and made some changes. She gave up her spot in Counterparts to become the female singer for the house band of an all-male performing troupe called Mask and Wig. The name *Adam* began popping up in our conversations. He was a senior as well as the leader of the band.

"We're just friends. He has a girlfriend at Vassar," Kathryn said.

For a boy with a girlfriend at Vassar, he spent an awful lot of time with my daughter. I could tell how much Kathryn enjoyed his company, and I hoped she wouldn't be hurt.

I woke up one night in time to hear Rick mumble "Ok" and then hang up the phone. He fell asleep before I could even check the time. It was three o'clock in the morning. I gave him a hard shove and asked who had called.

"It was Suzie. She said Kathryn was all right."

He pulled the covers up to his neck, adjusted his pillow and began falling asleep. I gave him another shove.

"What do you mean she's all right? Why wouldn't she be all right?"

Rick groaned and turned over.

"Suzie said Kathryn might have had too much to drink, but she's all right now."

He closed his eyes before he even finished the sentence. I wasn't getting anywhere with him, so I phoned Suzie.

"Suzie? What's going on?"

"Well, we had a birthday party for Kathryn, and she might have had a little too much to drink. You don't need to worry though because Adam's going to stay with her and make sure she's all right."

Adam? He seemed to be everywhere Kathryn was. Her life was in his hands, and I didn't even know his last name.

"Suzie, if Kathryn is all right, why did you call?"

"I didn't want to, but she made me. She said she wouldn't go to sleep unless I called to tell you she was okay. She was all right until she drank something blue Michael mixed. That's when she got sick."

I shook my head and glanced at Rick. At least one of us was sleeping peacefully. Before hanging up, I made Suzie promise to call if Kathryn needed help.

I lay on my pillow and stared at the ceiling. In her four years at Penn, Kathryn had seldom caused us a moment's worry. She was twenty-two now and about to graduate. Why had she acted so irresponsibly and put herself in danger? I tried to sleep but couldn't. I knew I would be awake all night, so I turned on the lamp and picked up a book. If no one called before morning, I would know she was all right.

The phone rang at seven o'clock and jolted me awake. I grabbed it and heard a weak voice say, "Mom, please come get me. I'm sick."

"You're not sick. You have a hangover."

"You can say anything you want, but please come get me."

"Be ready in twenty minutes."

Rick was still asleep - or dead. I didn't have time to find out which.

In West Philadelphia, the streets of row houses closest to campus are silent at seven a.m. on a Sunday morning, but you could fill a dumpster with the trash and empty bottles left from the previous night's escapades. It was with grave reservations Rick and I allowed Kathryn to move off-campus following her sophomore year.

I turned on 41st Street and parked in front of the three-story row house Kathryn shared with Suzie and six other girls. She was standing on the porch, and when she heard my car stop, she opened her eyes and began a slow descent down the front steps. She was wearing pajamas and an old gray robe. Her eyes were only half-open, and she was holding a mixing bowl under her mouth. Her long hair was disheveled and matted – no doubt from puke. When she reached the car, she opened the door and fell into the back seat.

"Mom, I know you have a lot to say, but could it wait until later?"

"I don't have anything to say. We've known each other a long time, and anything I might want to say, you've already heard. I'm here because you called. After seeing the way you look, I doubt you'll be trying anything like this again."

"I'm sorry, Mom. It won't happen again."

"Do what you know is right, Kathryn. You won't regret it."

As I pulled the car away from the curb and headed for home, I remembered my mother's words:

"Don't worry. It could be a lot worse."

It wasn't long before I found out exactly how much worse.

DARK DAYS 28

The clock on the wall in the waiting room was impossible to ignore. I could hear the movement of its second hand all the way across the room. I had been staring at it for forty minutes. Was forty minutes a good sign or a bad one? I was desperate to know what was happening. Had I made the right decision in bringing Kathryn here? Could someone help her? Would she be all right?

I wanted to be hopeful, but my heart was twisted into knots that seemed to choke off my own breath. Every imaginable worst-case scenario was running through my mind. It had only been a year since Kathryn graduated from Penn, but everything had changed. If I could turn the clock back to that time, I would.

Penn's Class of 2002 graduated on a Monday morning in May. It wasn't difficult to spot Kathryn among the thousands of people gathered in the stadium. Like all Penn graduates, she and her seven housemates had thought of a plan for drawing attention to themselves. They marched onto the field carrying bright lime-green plastic plates high above their heads.

I felt tremendous joy and an overwhelming sense of gratitude that day. Second-guessing our decision to leave Nashville was a mental activity I frequently engaged in during our first years in Philly. Had our sacrifices been worth this experience? At that moment, I knew the answer was yes.

As I watched Kathryn graduate that morning, I thought my challenges and fears as a parent were over. She was a capable, secure and educated adult. She had arrived, and I was prepared to relinquish my role. I was unaware that in a few months she would need me more than ever. Her problem came from out of the blue and threatened her life before any of us knew what was happening. By the time I realized the seriousness of the situation, it had gone on far too long, but I was determined to rectify my mistake.

I left the room before the applause ended. After listening to a half-hearted information session about Penn and its application process, the seventy-five or so prospective students and parents in the audience were being more than generous. My enthusiasm for Penn was missing that day. At one point, I even caught myself staring at some leaves falling past one of the gothic style windows in the room. Generally, I stayed behind after an information session and made myself available for questions, but not today. Instead, I rushed back to my office and closed the door.

I was having trouble keeping my eyes open. I had barely slept the night before, and when I did manage to doze, I woke with a crushing sense of distress. My conversation on the phone with Kathryn that evening had confirmed my fear that something was terribly wrong. Knowing she was eight hundred miles away was unbearable.

Her first year of law school went well, and that summer she divided her time between internships in Philadelphia and New York. However, at the beginning of this fall semester, I noticed a change in her demeanor. She anguished over inconsequential matters such as when to go to the grocery store or what to fix for dinner. She expressed fears and worries that had no basis in reality. She read a book about an abused child and feared perhaps the same thing had happened to her but she had lost her memory of it. Trying to reason with her was useless. Occasionally, light broke through her darkness, but within a matter of days, her anxiety would reappear. Her life slowly became a hell of her own making - one in which panic attacks were so intense she was terrified of dying.

She and Adam had dated for over a year, but it was difficult for them to be together. Following graduation, he made a two-year commitment to serve as a paralegal in the Manhattan District Attorney's Office. Somehow, despite the long commute between New York and Nashville, they held their relationship together. I knew they were close, but even Adam was unable to ease her fears.

What was happening, and how did it start? Did I give her too little support or too much? What should I have done differently? If there were warning signs, I missed them.

Fall semester was almost over, and Kathryn was frightened she would not be able to sit through her exams. In law school, the final exam in each class determines your grade for the semester. Although serious, this problem paled in comparison to my concerns about her mental and emotional well-being. She was in a perpetual state of stress, and I had never been so worried about her.

I picked up the phone and dialed an agent at US Airways. I wanted to be on the next flight to Nashville. After spending weeks trying to think of a solution to Kathryn's problem, I finally accepted the truth - I had none. She needed professional help, and I was going to make sure she received it.

Considering how late it was when I arrived, the Nashville Airport was surprisingly busy. I exited the security area and scanned the crowd.

"Mom!"

I turned in the direction of her voice and had my worst fears confirmed. Had I not known it was Kathryn, I might have passed her by like a stranger. She was gaunt, and her beautiful auburn hair hung in oily strands around her face. A quick look at her clothes suggested she had pulled them from a pile on the floor. The moment I reached her, she threw her arms around me and began to cry. When she was calm, I sent her for the car while I retrieved my luggage.

I was glad for a moment alone to compose myself. I knew from our phone conversations that Kathryn was anxious and despondent, but her appearance shook me terribly. It took all the strength I could muster to sound reassuring.

The next morning, I opened my eyes and saw sunlight beaming through the curtains. When I opened the blinds, I was surprised to find it snowing. I had become accustomed to the gray winter days of the northeast. I cracked open the door of Kathryn's room and peeked inside. She looked peaceful, and I suspected it was the first good sleep she had in a long time. I shut the door quietly and looked around the apartment. A quick glance was all it took to bring me back to reality.

Kathryn had never been terribly neat, but she had never resorted to living in the kind of squalor I saw around me. Empty food containers, dirty dishes, pots and pans covered the kitchen counters and filled the sink. The refrigerator and pantry were empty, and the trash smelled like it had been sitting for weeks. Everywhere I looked, things were in disarray and pointed to a crisis.

"Mom, you don't have to do that."

I looked up from scrubbing the bathroom floor and smiled at Kathryn. She had been asleep for eleven hours.

"I thought I would do some cleaning until you woke up."

"I know how bad the apartment looks. I'm sorry it's such a mess. I mean to clean it, but by the time I get home I'm too tired to do anything but go to bed."

"Why don't you take a long shower, and then we'll go somewhere for breakfast. How about the Pancake Pantry? I haven't been there in years."

The Pancake Pantry was one of her favorite places, but the enthusiasm I expected was replaced by a muffled, "all right."

The snow on the roads made driving treacherous, and I was relieved when we finally arrived at the restaurant. By the time we were seated, it was close to noon, and there were only a handful of people inside. Kathryn took small bites of her breakfast as I gobbled down my second pancake.

We were not at the Pancake Pantry by accident. We were there because of its location - it is within minutes of Vanderbilt's Student Health Center. When we finished eating, I ordered coffee. While we waited for our server to return, I began a conversation I had been rehearsing since the night before.

"Kathryn, I know you don't like feeling the way you do. I've tried to help, but the truth is neither of us knows how to fix whatever is wrong. You've suffered for months, and I think it's time we sought professional help. Would you be willing to go to Student Health and see if they can arrange for you to see someone?"

My worst fear was that my suggestion would be met with an angry refusal, but fortunately, that didn't happen.

"Will you come with me?" she asked.

"Of course."

"Can we go now?"

The lump in my throat and the tears filling my eyes made it impossible to speak, so I nodded yes. When we stood up, I took her hand and held it until we reached the car.

We drove to Vanderbilt and parked. The Student Health Center isn't accessible by car, so we bundled up in preparation for the walk. As we trudged through the snow, she gripped my hand. That small gesture tore at my heart. She was a strong, independent person, and seeing her lean on me for strength spoke to how deeply she was hurting.

A few minutes later, we reached Student Health and climbed the steps to the front door. There was a sign taped to the window. The Center was closed until noon the following day. I looked at Kathryn and saw tears welling in her eyes. It had taken so much courage to come here for help, but she had found none. I tried to sound confident in spite of my disappointment.

"We'll just come back tomorrow. Maybe we can arrange something before your first class."

Even now, I can remember the sound our footsteps made as we walked back across campus through the snow. I knew each step was taking her further away from the help she needed. When we arrived home, I phoned the law school.

"I'm trying to explain why my daughter can't talk with you. I flew here from Philadelphia last night and found her in a terrible state. Until she gets professional help, she's going to need support."

Vanderbilt Law School's Dean of Students was firm and direct.

"As I said before, I understand the circumstances, but Kathryn is the only person I can speak with concerning a change in her exam schedule. She needs to call me immediately."

I hung up and fought back tears. I wasn't sure Kathryn was up to making such a call, but I knew she had to try. I went to her room and explained what had to be done. I was relieved when she reached for the phone and dialed the number I gave her. I quietly left the room and shut the door.

Allowing a student to reschedule a final exam is virtually unheard of, but that is exactly what Vanderbilt's Dean of Students did. She instructed Kathryn to take every exam for which she could prepare and any she was unable to take would be administered to her before the start of the next semester. It was a generous accommodation, and we were more than grateful.

Early the next morning, we drove back to Student Health. I took a seat in the waiting area while Kathryn checked in at the reception desk. She had just sat down when a nurse called her name and ushered her through the doorway. I had now been waiting for nearly an hour and was growing more anxious by the minute.

I heard the door open and saw Kathryn. She looked in my direction and gave me a slight smile. A smile - even a small one - was a good sign, a hopeful sign. She stopped at the reception desk and then joined me.

"The doctor said I have an anxiety disorder, but it can be managed with medication and counseling. He thinks it may be triggered when a multitude of things I can't control converge on me all at once. He said my excessive worrying is a way of avoiding what I can't control."

We were talking when a young doctor came over and introduced himself.

"Kathryn and I had a long conversation, and I think I can have her feeling better soon. Generalized Anxiety Disorder (GAD) develops slowly and often begins in young adulthood. It's usually worse under stress, and if the number of students we treat from the Law School is any indication, law school must produce plenty of that."

He turned to Kathryn and said, "This is a prescription for the medication we discussed. It's important to begin taking it right away. When anxiety disorders aren't treated, they can lead to depression. Remember, there is no need to suffer. You aren't alone. Around seven million people in this country are affected by GAD."

Now that we knew what we were dealing with and had help, I knew Kathryn would be all right. We both needed a long cry to wash away all the fear from the past several days, but that would have to wait until later.

We discovered the temperature had warmed when we stepped outside, and most of the snow had melted. The sidewalks through campus were clear and made our walk back to the car an easy stroll. It seemed fitting for the sun to be shining at that moment.

Kathryn began the medication prescribed and completed all her exams on schedule. She graduated from Vanderbilt University Law School in 2005 and worked successfully for six years as an associate attorney for Shearman & Sterling LLP, first in their D.C. office and later in Manhattan. These days, when anxiety rears its ugly head, rather than allow it to zap joy from her life, she consults her doctor and brings it quickly under control.

Acknowledging I couldn't help Kathryn turned us toward someone who could. More importantly, her refusal to allow demeaning labels to prevent her from seeking and accepting help started her down the road to recovery. These were lessons I would always remember.

THE MAJOR GENERAL AND THE POET 29

Kathryn improved quickly, and I flew back to Philly. I arrived just in time for an announcement at Penn that, in typical fashion, defied logic. It was mind-boggling that common sense should be so uncommon at Penn.

I shut down my computer, grabbed my purse and headed for the door. I should have been at the White Dog Café twenty minutes ago. Rick and I often met there for dinner but never this early. I wondered if it had anything to do with the announcement concerning the hiring of his new boss, Major General Clifford Stanley, Commanding General, U.S. Marine Corps Combat Development Command.

Maj. Gen. Stanley's appointment as Penn's new executive vice-president provoked an immediate onslaught of criticism. Open skepticism of his qualifications to lead a major research institution threatened to thwart his authority before he even arrived on campus.

The position of executive vice-president had been vacant since the previous year when Rick's former boss, John Fry, resigned to become the fourteenth president of Franklin and Marshall College. At that time, President Rodin assumed leadership of Fry's direct reports. It seemed like a simple and logical solution, but that alone should have raised a red flag. Nothing simple or logical ever succeeded at Penn.

Penn's senior executives were some of the most highly regarded and sought after leaders in higher education. As such, they were neither afraid to voice their opinions nor exert their influence. Following Fry's departure, collegiality deteriorated, and administrators, vying for expanded responsibilities, became self-serving and confrontational. Unbeknownst to Maj. Gen. Stanley, he was about to enter a battlefield strewn with land mines... most of them strategically placed by his own troops.

Rick met weekly with President Rodin to update her on the status of audits within the university and the health system. During one of their meetings, she asked him to support Maj. Gen. Stanley with his transition. He assured her he would do everything possible to help. I knew his commitment would cost him dearly, and it did. His colleagues condemned his backing of Stanley.

I first met Cliff Stanley at a reception given in his honor shortly after he and his wife arrived at Penn. I had never met a nicer or more courteous person, and my heart went out to him. Regardless of his thirty years of military training, I knew Penn would chew him up and spit him out, and it did. Without the support of his staff, he was rendered ineffective. Twelve months after arriving, Maj. Gen. Stanley announced he was resigning his position to pursue other opportunities.

June 20, 2003 was a day Rick had dreaded for a long time. Following a scheduled meeting of the Board of Trustees, President Rodin announced she would be stepping down the next year. It would be difficult, if not impossible, to fill her shoes. During the decade in which she served Penn, its research funding doubled, and its endowment tripled. Its standing also rose in the U.S. News and World Report rankings from the sixteenth position among national universities to the fourth. More importantly, due to Penn's strategic investment in West Philadelphia, it was now a safe and vibrant community.

It had been the most exciting era in Penn's history, but Rick had accomplished everything he had come there to do, and he was ready for a different challenge. For the first time in years, he began returning calls to search firms. Over the next six months, he checked out a number of opportunities. A health-care system in Houston: too hot. A financial-services firm in Charleston: too bureaucratic. A technology company in Seattle: too far from our daughter, who was determined to move back to the Northeast as soon as she finished law school. Eventually, we grew weary of living in a state of limbo, and that, of course, was precisely when destiny knocked on our door.

It was a Tuesday morning, and like every weekday morning, I was sitting in my office reading Penn's student newspaper, the *Daily Pennsylvanian*. Starting the day before perusing it from cover to cover was to start the day one-step behind. Rick was also in his office that morning, but there was no time to glance through the paper. He had just received a call that would change our lives forever.

"You can't be serious," I said.

"It's true. I just got off the phone with a recruiter, and she wants to meet me in New York next week. What do you think?"

"New York? If the job were right, it could be an incredible opportunity."

"I think so, too. I'll let them know I'm coming."

I hung up the phone and leaned back in my chair. New York? I had dreamed of living there nearly all my life but never believed it would happen. Of course, one interview meant nothing. Pace University was recruiting an executive vice-president, and there were sure to be plenty of applicants. I went back to work, but the thought kept creeping into my mind. New York? No place on earth held more sway over my emotions. I could be packed and ready to go at a moment's notice.

Pace University's reputation did not precede itself, at least not outside the New York metropolitan area. Then again, it didn't hold itself out to be anything other than what it was - a university attempting to give students the opportunity to lift their lives and prospects. The similarities between Rick's life and the lives of numerous Pace students was not lost on him. Many students at Pace represent the first generation of their family to attend college. Rick, himself a first-generation college student, paid his way through college with a series of part-time jobs. He selected accounting as his major because it was a practical means of gaining a better, more secure future for himself and, ultimately, his family. He understood the motivation of the students who came to Pace and the importance of expanding their education. When he was offered the job, he didn't hesitate to accept.

We were excited about our move to Manhattan but in a quandary over where to live. It could take several months to transition from Philadelphia, and Rick had committed to starting work within thirty days. Kathryn suggested we direct our attention to *Craigslist*, a new classified advertising website. A few days later, I sat at the computer, pulled up the website and entered our criteria. Within seconds, a list of over two hundred apartments flashed before me. I skimmed the list and settled on a studio apartment on West 58th Street. I emailed an inquiry and continued browsing. A few minutes later, the phone rang. I picked it up and heard the melodic voice of a young Brazilian. Her name was Luciana and she was responding to my email.

"I was surprised to get your message. I only posted my ad ten minutes ago." (I resisted my natural urge to take this as a sign that it was meant to be.)

Luciana explained she was leaving New York at the end of the month to spend the fall in Brazil with her family. Her boyfriend, who we later learned was from Nashville, convinced her to sublet her condominium for three months while she was away. In spite of his encouragement, she was understandably apprehensive about renting her home to strangers. When Rick and I volunteered to drive to New York and meet with her, she sounded relieved.

That afternoon, despite a torrential rainstorm, we drove to New York and went to Luciana's apartment. I will never understand how two people, clueless about living in Manhattan, managed within two hours to stumble upon such a jewel. It's hard to say which of us was more relieved when we signed the lease.

Luciana's condominium exceeded our expectations. It was in an attractive building with a door attendant and sat just one block from the new Time Warner Center at Columbus Circle. Multiple subway stations and bus stops were within a short five-minute walk. To make Rick's transition easier, Luciana offered to leave everything in the apartment for Rick's personal use. The only thing he would need to bring to New York was his clothes.

The next Monday, Rick informed Dr. Amy Gutmann, who earlier that year succeeded Dr. Rodin as Penn's president, he would be leaving Penn at the end of September. I notified the Office of Undergraduate Admissions that I would be departing at the end of November. I knew Rick would devote little time to anything other than Pace for the next few months, and I thought staying behind in Philadelphia to coordinate our move would make the transition easier. It did but at the expense of being separated. I rectified my mistake by taking a train every Friday after work from 30th Street Station in Philadelphia to Penn Station in New York.

The first time I made the trip, I arrived at Penn Station around eight o'clock. Once I got my bearings, I rolled my suitcase to the apartment on 58th Street. I was searching for my key when the door opened.

"Where have you been?" Rick demanded. "It's ten o'clock. I've been pacing the floor for two hours."

"Where have I been? Where do you *think* I've been? I was on the train for two hours and then spent another hour walking here."

He looked surprised.

"You walked here from Penn Station? Why didn't you take a cab?"

"I didn't know where to get one, and asking would make me look like an unsophisticated newcomer."

"You *are* an unsophisticated newcomer. We both are."

He shook his head, pulled me inside and shut the door. The last thing he said before we fell asleep in each other's arms was that first thing the next morning, he would show me how to catch a cab.

It was Friday afternoon, and like every Friday for the past two months, I was taking the train to New York. However, this trip was different; I would not be coming back. I shut down my computer and stared at the empty screen. I needed to leave if I was going to catch my train, but I hesitated. Once I left my desk and walked out of College Hall, it was over.

There had been a thousand times I'd wished I was anywhere other than where I was, but now that it was time to go, it was hard to say goodbye. It was hard to file away nine years of memories. Only a few people knew my departure date, and I asked them not to share it. If there is an easy way to say goodbye, I have never found it. This particular parting was laced with enormous emotion, and just getting through the day had been much harder than I anticipated.

Years ago, I would never have imagined this day would be so painful. I originally resented everything about our move to Philadelphia. Assimilating into an unfamiliar culture in a different part of the country was daunting. Yet, in spite of those challenging first years and regardless of the hard knocks I took, living and working here was exactly what I needed in order to grow.

I picked up my purse, grabbed the handle of my suitcase and headed towards the door. As I pulled my bag along the hall, an unexpected memory flashed through my mind. I was standing on the porch of Eisenlohr Hall, the magnificent house that has been home to Penn presidents since the early eighties. It was the night before Penn's 244th commencement, and I was attending a dinner for that year's honorary degree recipients.

The commencement speaker was Nobel Laureate Seamus Heaney, the Ralph Waldo Emerson Poet in Residence at Harvard University and a former poetry professor at Oxford. At that time, his recent translation of the epic poem *Beowulf* was one of the bestselling books in Great Britain.

It was late, but the party at Eisenlohr was in full swing. In an attempt to revive myself, I ducked outside for some fresh air. I walked to the edge of the porch and looked out across the lawn. I heard something behind me and realized I wasn't alone. I turned and looked into the smiling face of Seamus Heaney. He was dressed in an ill-fitting dark suit and smoking a cigarette. His mop of white hair was damp with sweat, and his eyes danced.

"Would you care for a smoke?" he asked.

"No, thanks. I just came outside to get some fresh air."

"I know what you mean. There's a lot of hot air in there."

I smiled at his sense of humor.

"Tell me something," he asked. "What do you think of this place? Is it as great as they say?"

"Most people think so."

"What do you think?"

"I think the way you feel about a place depends on how you experience it."

"Ahhh...there's truth in what you say."

He smiled and took another drag on his cigarette. When he finished, he snuffed it out under his foot.

"I'd best be getting back inside. Will you join me?" he asked.

"No, I think I'll stay out here a while longer."

He nodded goodbye and rejoined the festivities. I had no doubt his presence was missed.

I maneuvered my suitcase through the last door of College Hall and headed toward 30th Street Station. When I reached the corner, the traffic light turned red. While I waited for it to change, I glanced over my shoulder at Penn's campus and thought of the words I said to Heaney. *The way you feel about a place depends on how you experience it.*

My association with Penn was complicated – the epitome of a classic love/hate relationship. Still, the same opportunities I once resisted led to some of the most extraordinary and unforgettable experiences I would ever have.

My eyes filled with tears, but I wouldn't allow them to fall. I was determined to walk away smiling. The light turned green, and I moved on.

EBAY'S AUCTION BLOCK

30

The clip-clop of hooves on West 57th Street created the illusion of waking up during the 1800s in old London town. The last thing I expected to hear in Manhattan was the sound of horse-drawn carriages clattering past my window. In spite of how noisy they sometimes were, I cherished my morning glimpses of these noble creatures. They were participants in one of New York's most time-honored traditions—hauling weary tourists through the city's most beloved venue, Central Park.

I reached for my calendar and tried to make sense of the hastily written notes I had scribbled the day before. I had an appointment at one thirty with our real estate agent, Carol. Securing housing in Manhattan is next to impossible without the help of a broker. Fortunately, the other party in our transaction would pay her generous finder's fee.

I arrived at Carol's office early and used the time to peruse information on the properties we planned to tour. One of the listings was particularly appealing. Its location on West 67th Street between Columbus Avenue and Broadway was ideal. Central Park is one block east and Lincoln Center two blocks south. There was just one problem. The apartment was privately owned, and the rental agreement would inevitably carry a clause allowing the owner to give notice and sell the property at any time. I refused to place myself in such a vulnerable position.

The apartments Carol and I toured were located all across the city: uptown, downtown, East Side, West Side, SoHo, NoHo, Murray Hill and the Village. After four exhausting hours, I needed a break. We passed a small coffee shop, and I suggested we stop and rethink our strategy.

"I believe what you're looking for is an apartment just like the one on West 67th Street. I know you have reservations about renting a privately owned apartment, but this one is different. Before we left my office, I spoke with the attorney who handles the property. The owner lives in London. Three years ago, he bought two apartments in the building—one for each of his daughters."

"How does that change anything? If one of them needed the apartment, we'd still have to move."

"True, but it's going to be a long time before that happens. The attorney told me the daughters are only four and six."

I grabbed my purse and headed for the door.

"I'm right behind you," Carol yelled.

We phoned from our cab and arranged to view the apartment. When we pulled up in front of the building, a uniformed door attendant rushed to our assistance. His muscular physique convinced me he could handle anyone or anything threatening the sanctuary of that building.

Gilbert, the concierge, greeted us and handed Carol a key to apartment 27 K. He was charming, professional and had a smile I would look forward to seeing each morning. As Carol and I rode the elevator to the 27th floor, I had a feeling this would be my next home.

I tried to be patient while Carol fiddled with the key.

"I can't get the top lock to work. Why don't you keep trying, and I'll go downstairs and ask for another key," she said before rushing off.

I took out my lip-gloss, rubbed some on the key (a handy trick I learned in my youth) and turned the lock. The first thing I noticed when

I stepped inside was the light. The windows faced west, and the sunset bathed the walls in a soft, pink glow.

The view was spectacular. Below was bustling Broadway, and The Juilliard School and Lincoln Center were on my left. If I sat on the window sill and leaned far enough, I could even glimpse the George Washington Bridge. The crowning glory of this incredible vista was the Hudson River. True, I could only see a small piece of it—the piece visible between two high-rise buildings on Broadway—but even so, I could watch sailboats and barges pass.

"The rent is six thousand eight hundred dollars a month (more than three times our last mortgage), and a six thousand dollar deposit is required. Of course, they'll need to run a background check on both of you, verify your income and personal assets and will want at least three references," Carol explained.

"We'll take it. Just tell me how to start the process."

"Won't Rick want to see the apartment before you sign a letter of intent?"

"Trust me. He'll love it as much as I do."

Fortunately, he did. Three weeks later, we stuffed our clothes in the car, left a thank-you note on Luciana's kitchen table and moved into our nine hundred square feet of high-rise bliss. It was official: we were New Yorkers, and we had a lease and cable bill to prove it.

A few weeks later, I was talking with a neighbor from across the hall when he asked if either Rick or I played the piano.

"No, neither of us does. I wish we did. Why do you ask?"

"I was just curious. The last tenant in your apartment was Alexa Joel, Billy Joel's daughter. She lived here while she was studying at Juilliard. It took a while to get used to her piano practice. I must say, I don't miss it."

Billy Joel? The piano man? His daughter lived in my apartment. I adore Billy Joel. I did everything short of selling my soul to get tickets to his performance at Penn. I remembered the letters I had been returning to our mailroom. The name Alexa Joel had not registered with me. Billy Joel. Who would have thought that one day I would be forwarding his daughter's mail?

The thrill of being in such close proximity to fame eventually waned. Even the awe provoking sight of Liam Neeson, who lived in the apartment above us, gradually lost its luster once I began riding the elevator to the lobby each morning with him and his two sons. In no time at all, he became just an average Joe who reminded his boys to work hard at school.

Possibly due to the city's excessive number of self-proclaimed V.I.P.s, celebrity status receives far less attention in New York than in other places. However, New Yorkers still enjoy boasting of the luminaries living in their buildings. Those of us on the 27th floor of *my* building were proud to have Tony Danza living at the end of our hall. Friendly and courteous, he was an ideal neighbor. His apartment was located next to the elevator and each morning I was treated to the mellow sounds of his trumpet. Scarcely a day passed that he wasn't up early practicing his music or exercising at the gym. Prior to his acting career, he was a boxer and still worked out religiously.

We were both in the elevator late one afternoon when he asked about my plans for the evening.

"Oh, nothing really. I'm on my way to get a manicure. After that, I'm coming home and catching up on the last three days of the *Times*. How about you? It looks like you're headed for the gym."

His face dropped and his shoulders slumped.

"No, I'm meeting up with some friends at a bar on 79th and then going to a party."

I cringed. It was difficult to tell when Tony was dressed *up* or dressed *down* because he always wore black. Nonetheless, it was a tactless blunder impossible to rectify without adding to the embarrassment. When the elevator reached the lobby, I stepped off, but Tony stayed on.

"Did you forget something?" I asked.

"No, I just need to go back upstairs for a minute."

The elevator doors closed, and I quickly exited the building. I wondered how many years I would have to live in New York to acquire even an ounce of *savoir-faire*.

Not long after moving into our apartment, one of the most famous art exhibits in New York's history arrived in our neighborhood and I spent as much time as possible enjoying it. *The Gates* was a temporary exhibit by renowned artists Christo and Jeanne-Claude. They spent two decades fighting the city for permission to display their extraordinary work in Central Park. Fortunately, when Michael Bloomberg became mayor, Christo and Jeanne-Claude gained an ally.

For the past month, I had watched workers install 7,500 vinyl gates along Central Park's twenty-three miles of pathways. Each gate stood sixteen feet tall and varied in width from five to eighteen feet. When unfurled, the saffron-colored fabric panels suspended from the frames were designed to resemble a river of gold meandering through the bare winter landscape of the park.

In reality, the gates themselves bore a strong resemblance to large metal doorframes, and the fabric panels were akin to the shade of orange worn by hunters during deer season. When viewed from above or at a distance, *The Gates* looked less like a golden river than it did a colossal set of orange dominos. However, none of that mattered. *The Gates* was stunning in the otherwise bleak winter terrain of Central Park. Admirers received an extra bonus when a nor'easter hit the city and blanketed it with snow. This pristine setting made *The Gates* even more spectacular.

The Gates was my first exposure to the unparalleled cultural delights of New York. In days to come, I'd find myself mesmerized by The Metropolitan Museum of Art, the New York Philharmonic, the City Ballet and the Metropolitan Opera, but it's *The Gates* that I'll never forget. Similar to New Yorkers, it was bold, unique and demanded attention.

The Gates remained on display for sixteen days. When volunteers began dismantling the installation, I went to the park for one final look. I was sitting on Literary Walk when a staff member strolled over to talk. I told him how much I had enjoyed *The Gates* and wished it could stay longer. Before going back to work, he reached in his pocket and handed me a small orange swatch he had cut from one of the panels.

"Keep this. It might be worth something one day," he said.

When I got back to the apartment that afternoon, I placed the cloth in my box of keepsakes. That tiny bit of fabric would help me remember walking through the snow and watching 7,500 orange panels swaying in the breeze.

Several months ago, I showed my small swatch to a friend who said she had seen similar ones sell for ten dollars on eBay.

"That might be worth some real money one day," she said.

Before going to bed that night, I took the piece of orange fabric from my box of keepsakes, rubbed it between my fingers and recalled a crisp fall night when Rick and I strolled together through *The Gates*. How much is that memory worth? More that I could ever get from eBay's auction block.

CITY OF CONCRETE AND STEEL 31

New York is an expensive place to live, and there was a limit to how long my freedom could last. Rick began leaving not-so-subtle hints around the apartment: a brochure under my pillow announcing an upcoming job fair at the local Y, a copy of *How to Find the Perfect Job in Thirty Days or Less* placed strategically next to my coffee mug. He even managed to find an old copy of my resume and left it taped in the middle of our bathroom mirror. At last, I surrendered and began my search.

The only thing more dispiriting than looking for a job is looking for a job and not finding one. My next few months in Manhattan were consumed with applying for any position for which I was remotely qualified. It wasn't easy trying to convince the American Red Cross I was capable of coordinating its preparedness program while at the same time persuading the Development Office of Lincoln Center I was uniquely gifted in the art of fundraising. Both organizations deserve credit for seeing through my somewhat inflated resume.

When I wasn't busy conjuring up schemes to secure a job, I wandered around Lincoln Square or the Upper West Side. The observations I made during those walks served me well. First, there was no need to waste time going to a grocery. The trucks from Fresh Direct, parked on every other street, directed me to a website where, with the simple click of my mouse, I could shop for food, health or beauty products, select my delivery time and sit back and wait for my doorman to announce their arrival. All the local dry cleaners picked up at my building and offered same day delivery. As for meals, I could order anything from yellowfin tuna ribbons to foie gras brûlée delivered to my door in thirty minutes or less.

Within two blocks of my apartment, I discovered a post office, nail salon, shoe repair shop, farmers' market, bar, drugstore, coffee house, four gourmet restaurants, diner, furniture outlet, dry cleaners, clothing boutique, bookstore, grocery, movie theatre, church, exercise facility, hardware store and vitamin shop. When it comes to convenience, Manhattan is without equal.

Except for Central Park, nature in the city consists primarily of skinny trees planted in the medians of major avenues. Rather than provide shelter or a welcomed breeze on a hot day, their main function appeared to be capturing stray plastic bags blowing aimlessly about the street. As far as wildlife is concerned, apart from freshly groomed pets, I rarely spotted anything on the Upper West Side—except for the hawk.

I was walking up Broadway one morning when I happened to look up and catch sight of a hawk enjoying a breakfast of pigeon on a second-floor windowsill. Others followed my stare, and within moments, photos of the hawk were traveling through cyberspace. A crowd gathered, and people began mingling. A young man dressed in a black Armani suit started a conversation with two construction workers. An elderly lady chatted with a couple of tattooed teens from a nearby high school, and when a woman standing next to me learned I was new to the city, she presented me with her card.

"I'm in real estate. Call if I can be of any help," she said.

Moments later, the crowd parted, and I was left on the corner to ponder what I had just witnessed. The hawk's presence had an extraordinary effect. To this day, I have never seen anything tear down as many social barriers in such a short amount of time as that single sighting of nature in a city of concrete and steel.

It's difficult to stay in touch with nature when you live in an urban environment as large as New York City. A number of years after moving to Manhattan, Rick and I were lying on the rooftop deck of our health club one night when I noticed a strange light in the sky. I pointed it out and asked his opinion.

"What do you think it is? I've been watching it, and it hasn't moved."

Jets streamed back and forth across the sky, but the light remained stationary.

"I'm not sure what it is," Rick said. "Wait a minute. Is it a star?"

"A star? I think you're right. I haven't seen one in a long time."

We lay quietly watching the night sky and listening to the street musician next to Barnes and Noble play his horn. I was the first to break the silence.

"Promise me something. Promise me we won't die in Manhattan. I want to die in a place where I can look up and still see more stars than planes."

"Agreed."

A few minutes later, I fell asleep. It was the most peaceful sleep I had had in a long time.

I found New York infinitely intriguing and always thought of Rick when I was out walking. He loved investigating the city as much as I did, but free time was a luxury he didn't have. As he began analyzing Pace's finances, it became apparent the situation was far more serious than anyone realized. He found himself juggling credit ratings, restructuring debt and fending off bond insurers. I still recall how elated he was the day Merrill Lynch granted the university an unsecured loan of sixty-six million dollars. It was a major coup.

Rick's hectic schedule troubled me. He rarely made it home before nine o'clock and even then spent several hours responding to emails. When I complained about his 24/7 Blackberry usage, he took to concealing it. It didn't take long to realize his new penchant for watching movies in the dark was simply a maneuver to hide his phone.

His workload was not the only thing that concerned me. He had always shown tremendous discipline concerning exercise and diet. Now, however, they appeared to be his last priority. The Reebok Club, located next door to our building, is without question one of the best health clubs in Manhattan. After moving into our apartment, Rick immediately purchased a membership. I frequently reminded him that carrying a membership card in his wallet did not constitute a workout.

Even worse than his lack of exercise was his total disregard for his diet. During the week, his dinner seldom consisted of anything more than a glass of wine and a plate of cheese. He was his own worst enemy; he cared too much, and he sacrificed too much. I gave up complaining and left him to himself. He would either find the success he was seeking or self-destruct. Responsibility for shoring up the university rested heavily on his shoulders.

I came home one day and found the light on our answering machine blinking. I punched the play button and proceeded to hang up my jacket. Five seconds into the message, I dropped my coat and sat down.

"If you're still interested, please give me a call."

The message was from the United Methodist Committee on Relief (UMCOR), a global humanitarian aid organization of The United Methodist Church. Its headquarters is in Manhattan, and there was an opening for a program assistant. It was my first choice among all the jobs for which I had applied. I returned the call to the Director of Human Resources and made an appointment for Friday. I was nervous. I had never worked for this kind of agency and wasn't sure how to even prepare for the interview.

I wanted to make a good impression, so I allowed myself plenty of time to dress on Friday. Unfortunately, it didn't help as much as I had hoped. I sucked in my stomach, threw back my shoulders and smiled. It was no use. The kindest word I could think of to describe the person staring back at me from the mirror was *frumpish*. In spite of my weekend fasting and the new suit I was wearing, I definitely looked like a woman past her prime. I wasn't sure when or how it happened, but since it could not be rectified in the next forty-five minutes, I grabbed my purse and headed for the subway. Twenty minutes later, I reached 116th Street, found my way to the Office of Human Resources and met Ms. Williams, the Assistant Director.

"This is a two-part interview," said Ms. Williams. "Today, I'd like to hear about your past work experience and then have you perform a typing test on the computer. After all candidates for this position have been evaluated, several will be invited back to meet with UMCOR's Assistant Deputy General Secretary."

Did I hear her correctly? Did she say *typing test*? I hadn't heard that term used since the seventies. As we talked, I sensed UMCOR made good use of its resources, but its systems and procedures were sorely outdated.

When our meeting ended, Ms. Williams led me to a small cubicle outside her office. On the desk sat an old keyboard attached to a monitor anchored high above. The computer reminded me of one Rick and I purchased back in '82.

"When you're ready to begin, just touch any key, and the test will start. The instructions are on the screen."

With that said, Ms. Williams turned and left me with the ancient relic she had referred to as a computer. I put on my reading glasses and stared at the keyboard. Then I took my reading glasses off and scrutinized the screen over-head. Back and forth, repeatedly. In order to see both the keyboard and the monitor I had to continually adjust my glasses. It was impossible to concentrate. Ms. Williams returned shortly and asked if I was finished.

"Yes, but I don't think I did very well. The height of the monitor made it difficult to see."

"Don't worry. I'm sure you did fine."

She was wrong. I had not done well, and I knew it. I had blown my only chance at the one job in New York I truly wanted.

For a long time, I had felt an urging in my heart to give more of myself to others - the poor, the sick, the lonely and the desperate. I knew working for UMCOR would help satisfy that longing. Its mission is to help alleviate suffering for the world's most vulnerable people. I had hoped to be a part of that undertaking.

I walked back to the subway to catch the downtown train. It was early afternoon, and the station was deserted. The dim lights overhead and the dank odor of the tunnel added to my gloom. I knew the right job would eventually come along, but at that moment, my disappointment was overwhelming.

Staying busy lifts my spirits, so following my unfortunate interview, I spent the next several days reorganizing our small apartment. I was excited to try the vacuum-sealed storage bags I had seen advertised on television. I was leery of the claim they could triple my storage space, but I ordered three packages anyway.

The storage bags arrived two days later, and I went to work. I placed ten of Rick's polo shirts in a bag, connected the bag to our vacuum cleaner and turned it on. Right before my eyes, the bag compressed into a ten-inch square with a depth of only three inches. It was incredible.

I used my new purchase on all our seasonal clothes and then stored them under the couch in our living room. It worked perfectly. In fact, it worked too well. After a while, we forgot the clothes were under the couch and accused our dry cleaner of losing them. Two years later, I dropped a grape that rolled under the couch, and we rediscovered our lost apparel. Styles had changed by that time, so we donated everything to Goodwill. The clerk accepting the donation looked skeptical when I handed her five small plastic bags and asked for a receipt for eleven shirts, three pairs of slacks, six blouses and a cardigan.

Although the lack of storage in our apartment was frustrating, the experience of living in a small space was invaluable. It reminded me of the difference between need and want. I found it liberating to live with so few possessions.

The phone was ringing when I opened the door one day not long after my organizing binge, and I rushed to answer it.

"Hello?" I panted.

"Is this Nancy?"

"Yes."

"Nancy, this is Kristen Sachen. I am the Assistant Deputy General Secretary of UMCOR, and I'm calling to see if you might be available to meet with me sometime this week to discuss the position in which you expressed interest."

I was speechless. Was this some sort of joke? It didn't sound like a joke.

"I would welcome the opportunity to speak with you," I said.

We worked out the details and said good-bye. I was dumbfounded. Why would anyone at UMCOR consider me for a job after seeing the results of that awful test? I knew I had performed miserably. Was it possible my poise or communication skills outweighed the results? It wasn't likely. Whatever the reason, I was grateful for another chance.

Two days later, I met with Kristen in her office. We talked extensively about UMCOR and ways I could contribute to its mission. In her role as Assistant Deputy General Secretary, Kristen oversaw every project at UMCOR, both domestically and abroad. She was inundated with work and needed an assistant who would not require a lot of oversight. I knew we would work well together because I hate being managed. Kristen offered me the job, and I accepted. Before our meeting ended, I couldn't help but comment on the typing test.

"I want you to know I'm much more proficient on the computer than my typing test indicates. The overhead monitor used during the test was difficult to see."

Kristen sighed and shook her head.

"The test and computer are both obsolete. I'm afraid you will find many things here are very outdated, but I hope it won't discourage you. Little by little, change is taking place."

She examined a folder on her desk and smiled.

"Your score on the test was about average, but your difficulty with the monitor might explain why you checked you were a citizen of the United Kingdom."

I thanked Kristen and left before she could rethink her decision. When I got outside, I turned on Broadway and found myself standing in a sea of diversity. The throng of distinct nationalities visible from that single corner was remarkable. My mind flashed back to a night years before when Joey and I stood on the corner of West Fourth Street and Sixth Avenue and watched hundreds of young people dressed in outlandish costumes rebel against the status quo. Manhattan is no longer the breeding ground for civil disobedience it once was, but it's still a city that encourages liberal thinking, treasures diversity and isn't afraid to call discrimination by its name.

I reached the entrance to the subway and ran down the steps to catch the next downtown train. I was beyond elated. I had a job – an opportunity to make a difference. I thought about Kristen's last words as I left her office. *The hours will be long but rewarding.*

I couldn't think of a better way to spend my life.

GOD'S HOLD ON ME

32

We seek to love God above all things and our neighbors as ourselves. I found it impossible to pass the church on the corner of 60th Street and Park Avenue without noticing the words on the sign outside its door. Loving God above all things is the crux of the Christian faith, and loving one's neighbor as one's self is fundamental to being a follower of Christ. I have a genuine desire to be charitable and show kindness, but in a large urban city like New York, safety necessitates keeping your guard up at all times. This juxtaposition between faith and caution wasn't easy to reconcile.

I woke one Sunday morning to a clear blue sky and decided to pay Christ Church a visit. Rick was out of town, so this would give me a chance to investigate on my own. If I walked through Central Park, I could be there in less than thirty minutes.

Except for the occasional jogger or dog walker, the pathways through the park were deserted. My heavy coat and wool gloves helped fend off the chill of early spring. As I walked along, I found myself recalling Sunday mornings when I was a child. My mother was adamant about attending church, and if I complained, she said it was a sign the devil was trying to get a hold on me. The image her statement created was all it took to get me in my Sunday best.

I arrived at 60th and Park Avenue and entered the sanctuary through a pair of teak wood doors. I was unprepared for the splendor surrounding me. I glanced through a brochure I picked up by the door and read that the Venetian mosaics in the sanctuary are considered equal to the finest Byzantine art in the world. Although the space around me was exquisite, what truly captured my attention was the diversity of the congregation. The young sat among the old, and both black and white escorted visitors to their seats. Holy Communion was offered to everyone present and church members extended their hand to every guest.

Even before the choir finished the last stanza of "Here I Am Lord," I knew this was where I belonged. The moment I stepped off Park Avenue and walked through the doors of the church, I felt at home. The beauty surrounding me had nothing to do with it. God was in the house, and I could feel it as tangibly as the wooden pew beneath me. It was evident in the sermon and on the faces of everyone seated around me. I had stumbled into a Park Avenue church grand enough for kings but with the heart and soul of a servant.

I met some of the most interesting people I have ever known at Christ Church and made some of the best friends I have ever had. Several years after joining the church, Reverend Bauman asked if I would consider serving as the congregation's lay leader. As a lifelong member of the United Methodist Church, I was familiar with the responsibilities of the role, but I still sought clarification so I did some research.

The Lay Leader should be a living example of one who loves God and neighbor. Hmm . . . I love God and care about others, but I wasn't sure I did either well enough to qualify as a living example.

A Lay Leader should be a growing Christian disciple who understands that everyone has spiritual gifts and experiences that are vital to the Body of Christ. I was comfortable in crossing this one off the list. I am generally an inclusive person who embraces diversity and the contributions of others. The next line, however, gave me a reason to pause.

The Lay Leader is a role model to others for Christian discipleship lived out in daily life. I had no illusions about my qualifications as a role model. I needed one myself. I made up my mind to decline Reverend Bauman's offer but decided to wait until the next morning to give him a final answer.

By dawn, I had arrived at a different conclusion. For whatever reason, Reverend Bauman believed I was capable of serving as the lay leader for the congregation of Christ Church. I was not convinced he was right, but I knew he had faith I could do the job or he would not have asked.

This was a defining moment for me. Fear of failure had plagued me much of my life and swayed far too many of my decisions. Over time, I learned to avoid failure by refusing opportunities other than those at which I was sure I could succeed. If I moved outside my comfort zone, and replaced fear with trust in God, what would happen? It was time to find out. I accepted the job, prayed for faith equal to the task and trusted God to use my life to make a difference in someone else's.

Between my commitments at church and my duties at UMCOR, God seemed to have a hold on me. Everywhere I turned, I walked smack into the gospel. Nowhere was that truer than at UMCOR. Its work put the great commandment to "love your neighbor as yourself" into action every day.

My first experience in crisis management began with assisting survivors of the tsunami that had recently hit Indonesia. Food, water and medicine were dispatched to those affected, and over forty-four million dollars was raised for long-term relief efforts. UMCOR personnel traveled to Indonesia and returned with pictures and stories that haunted me for months. An estimated hundred and fifty thousand lives were lost.

There was quiet before the next storm, but it didn't last long. On August 29, 2005, Hurricane Katrina made landfall in southeast Louisiana and resulted in the costliest natural disaster in U.S. history. As scenes of the aftermath began airing on television, our phones rang incessantly with donors offering support.

In response to the enormous impact of the storm, UMCOR submitted a proposal to FEMA for a grant of sixty-six million dollars that would allow for two years of long-term recovery support for survivors of Katrina. It is impossible to know whether public outcry over FEMA's weak response to the disaster had any impact on their decision, but they quickly approved our proposal. News of the FEMA grant shocked humanitarian aid organizations. It was unheard of for a religiously affiliated entity to receive that kind of government support.

UMCOR used funds from the grant to establish a long-term case management program known as Katrina Aid Today (KAT). The objective of the program was to help restore lives and rebuild families by identifying their specific needs and helping facilitate access to resources.

I knew we faced enormous hurdles when our work first began, but I had no idea how much would ultimately be required. At its peak, the KAT consortium had one hundred and thirty-eight offices in thirty-four states and delivered approximately fifty million dollars in services to over one hundred and thirty thousand individuals.

I didn't tour New Orleans's Ninth Ward until a year after Katrina, but not much had changed. While my colleagues were investigating some abandoned cars, I wandered inside a house. A thick blanket of mud covered everything. A pair of loafers in front of a portable television in the living room and the dishes in the kitchen sink gave evidence the house was abandoned at a moment's notice. I found a doll lying on one of the beds and wondered about the people who once lived there. Did they watch the water flood their home and destroy their possessions? Where did they go? Where were they now?

Working for UMCOR taught me a great deal about the world. I learned to see myself in my neighbor, but it was a bitter lesson. Most of my neighbors are suffering, and to love them as much as I love myself requires more than acknowledging their pain. Love requires me to share in it.

BETTER THAN I EVER DREAMED 33

Following an intense year of scrutinizing accounting records and implementing change, Rick began catching small glimpses of the proverbial light at the end of the tunnel. The moment he did, I insisted he scale back his grueling schedule.

When it came to fun, our apartment was the perfect jumping off point. On any given night, we could attend a first-class performance at Lincoln Center, stop in Rosa Mexicano – home of the city's best pomegranate margarita – for dinner and drinks and then walk leisurely home by way of Central Park West. If our door attendants suspected we had enjoyed one too many margaritas, they would discretely ensure the elevator delivered us safely to our floor.

We never took our close proximity to Central Park for granted or the pleasures it ushered in with each new season. As the temperature rose and sun-worshipers reappeared in Sheep Meadow, Rick and I could be found lying on a blanket alongside ten thousand other New Yorkers at outdoor concerts featuring rising stars from the Metropolitan Opera.

Autumn seemed to appear out of nowhere and left behind its calling card of crimson and gold leaves for us to enjoy. I never cared for winter until we moved to New York, but once I experienced ice-skating on Wollman Rink, walking through The Ramble in the snow and watching children sled down the steps of Bethesda Fountain, it became a magical time of year. Even so, spring was always my favorite season. Almost overnight, the flowers, trees and bushes of Central Park would unfurl their colors and paint every pathway and hillside. The park was a place of peace in the middle of madness.

Depending on our mood, we might take the subway over to Queens and try out a new Greek restaurant or attend an off-Broadway show near Union Square. We sipped on herbal tea at Tea & Sympathy, shared lobster rolls at The Mermaid Inn and enjoyed Viennese hot chocolate at Café Mozart on cold winter nights. Regardless of what we wanted, it could always be found somewhere and usually at any hour of the day or night.

Lincoln Center gave me a new appreciation for the arts. From the first scene to the closing act, the grand Metropolitan Opera held me captive. Hearing the great violinist, Joshua Bell, perform with the New York Philharmonic was unforgettable.

Each summer Lincoln Center also becomes the setting for *Midsummer Night Swing*. Free musical entertainment and inexpensive swing dance lessons help fill the plaza. Dancing there on a warm summer evening offered unparalleled ambiance.

I was living my dream. Adventure lay right outside my door, yet within my apartment there existed peace and tranquility . . . at least for a while.

The phone rang late on a Tuesday night. It was Kathryn, who informed us she was unhappy with her work, Adam and the entire District of Columbia. She had contacted the New York office of her law firm and been offered a job starting Monday. If we didn't mind, she would move in with us on Friday night. In addition to her wine collection (six bottles of Riesling) and wardrobe, she would also be bringing her large Himalayan cat, Sassy.

"Of course we don't mind," I said as I pondered where her clothes could go, much less her cat. "It will be great having you here."

I hung up and looked at Rick. The newspaper he had been reading was in his lap, and he was staring at me with an open mouth.

"Is she moving in with us?" he asked.

"Only until she finds her own apartment. There's plenty of room."

He looked at me without speaking, and then went back to his newspaper. He would survive. We all would.

I went in our second bedroom and examined the closet to determine if there was even an inch of space for Kathryn's clothes. It was a preposterous idea. If an inch of available space existed, half of my clothes wouldn't be in plastic bags stuffed under the living room couch.

I sat down on the bed and thought back to the years when I was young and trying to figure out what to do with my life. Kathryn was at that point now, and she needed our support. It would be here when she arrived—along with a few over-the-door clothes hooks, a large litter box and some cat food.

True to her word, on Friday night around a quarter to eleven, Kathryn's car turned the corner at 67th street and pulled in front of our building. She arrived at our door holding her pillow and an extra-large pet carrier. She was followed by our door attendants, who deposited her clothes and collection of wine in our foyer and then quickly escaped.

"We're here," she announced with a big grin.

Did she think we hadn't noticed?

It's one thing to be entertained; it's quite another to be enlightened. My favorite moments are when the two come together. No experience typifies this more than *Inside the Actors Studio*.

Our association with *Inside the Actors Studio* and its indelible host, James Lipton (Jim), began in 2005 when the contract between The New School and the Actors Studio Drama School failed to be renewed. Pace administrators successfully negotiated bringing the school and the popular television show *Inside the Actors Studio* to the university's Schimmel Center. Rick, along with others, worked diligently to ensure the new collaboration went smoothly.

Recorded before a live audience consisting of Pace students and other guests, the show brings to the stage some of the most successful and highly regarded performers of all time. They come prepared to share their craft and their life experiences. As they speak, Jim masterfully cuts through the superficial and leads them into intimate territory. The shows are riveting and spontaneous, and despite long workdays, I tried to attend as many tapings as possible. Rick's office was located in the same building as the Schimmel Center, which made it possible for him to be there also.

Over time, certain themes became evident. Most of the guests who appeared on the show had endured harsh setbacks. The night Tim Allen appeared on the show, he talked about his arrest for drug trafficking at age twenty-five. His incarceration lasted two years, during which time he used comedy as a means of protection.

"Prison is where I fine-tuned my skills as a stand-up comic. If I could keep them laughing, they'd leave me alone."

He laughed along with the audience, but I suspect there was more fact than fiction in his comment.

The stories I heard deeply affected me. They revealed the means by which many of the performers overcame tremendous obstacles. Their stories were heart breaking but inspiring and instructive. The lessons shared were of determination and endurance, and I listened carefully to every word.

The first time Rick and I visited the Liptons' apartment on East 80th Street was to attend a holiday party for individuals associated with the Drama School. The collection of personal photographs covering their walls drew my attention. Nearly every celebrity and world leader from the past five decades stood posed next to Jim or his beautiful wife, Kedakai.

The party was still in full swing at midnight when Rick and I said good-bye and headed for the door. Before we walked out, I glanced over my shoulder and saw Jim sitting in his favorite chair surrounded by a group of enthralled students. As long as even one of them needed his attention, he would remain there.

Jim has done everything, been everywhere and has the resources to do whatever he wants, but what he chooses to do is help young acting students fulfill their dreams. He is more than just their mentor; he's their inspiration . . . theirs *and* mine.

I reached in the pocket of my coat and checked the address I had scribbled down on a scrap of paper earlier in the day. I was on my way to attend my friend Joan Ross Sorkin's first reading of her new play *Therapy, New York-Style*. Joan is a successful playwright whose incredible tenacity has kept her creative juices flowing for over twenty years. My exposure to the unique world of live theatre is due almost entirely to her.

Since my move to Manhattan, I had attended many readings similar to the one I was attending that night. The high price of space in Manhattan usually dictates they occur in obscure buildings in questionable parts of the city. If tonight's performance was similar to others I had attended, the reading would be held on an upper floor that may or may not be reachable by elevator, and someone stationed at a table outside the room would collect a small entrance fee to help cover expenses.

Getting to a reading might require some maneuvering, but it was always worth the effort. Listening as seasoned directors, writers and performers critique new works offers an extraordinary education. Joan taught me to appreciate the theatre for what she describes as "a place where thoughts are deeper, emotions rawer and astonishing surprises abound."

I found the address I was searching for, and someone buzzed me into the building. I was relieved to find a small elevator in the lobby and punched the button to the third floor. When I exited the elevator, I found myself in a small room where approximately twenty or so folding chairs were set up. A podium and a couple of additional chairs up front were the only designated stage. In spite of the cold weather, it was hot inside, and several men in the back of the room were struggling to open a window.

I waved to Joan, who was across the room giving last minute direction to the actor performing her work that evening. I saw her husband, Larry, seated on the front row and joined him. Larry's sharp intellect always ensured an engaging critique of a performance.

The first reading began around eight o'clock. The program that evening consisted of five original works being performed for the first time before a live audience. Joan's play was second on the program. It was provocative and well received. She had every reason to be pleased.

The third reading occurred right before intermission. The actor was British and a friend of the writer. The play began with the actor posing as an evangelical minister delivering a rousing sermon to his congregation as he, off-stage, consumed lots of hard liquor. The actor had no difficulty getting into his part. As he stood in front of us delivering his sermon, he grew louder, wilder and more enthused. Slowly, before my eyes, he began removing his clothes and masturbating. Fortunately, for his real audience, especially those of us seated on the front row, he was limited to the fifteen minutes allotted to the reading, so we were spared the climax of his performance.

There was an uncomfortable silence in the room, and I avoided looking at Larry. Joan glanced in my direction and rolled her eyes.

I remembered her words, "The theatre is a place where thoughts are deeper, emotions rawer and astonishing surprises abound."

I'm not sure how deep the actor's thoughts were, but he clearly had an abundance of raw emotion, and the reading definitely held surprises. This unpredictable nature of the theatre is what intrigues me and keeps me coming back. That, and the hope that I might be sitting in an audience one day when someone on stage stumbles upon the answers not only to their questions, but also to mine.

WORSE THAN I EVER IMAGINED 34

Rick and I often debate the concept of middle age. He likes to believe it's a stage of life in which we still hold membership, but I disagree. Fifty is not the new forty. It's fifty. Get over it.

Age has its virtues. For example, I'm more inclined to listen than speak and more generous in letting others have their way rather than insist on my own. Most importantly, age has taught me to take nothing for granted—nothing.

I resented turning forty, but age no longer bothered me. I was prepared to grow old, but ill prepared for the package that came with it. It showed up unexpectedly out of nowhere. I didn't want it and had done nothing to deserve it, but there it was. On an otherwise normal day, my whole world changed. It all started with a bag of popcorn.

My colleague Michael stood in the doorway sniffing the air.

"Someone's cooking popcorn," he said.

"I don't think so. I don't smell anything."

"Really? Well, someone is definitely cooking popcorn, and I want my share."

Michael laughed and disappeared down the hallway. He returned a few minutes later and handed me a bag of popcorn.

"Compliments of Joan. You should be glad I'm persistent," he said.

I was surprised. Popcorn has a strong odor. Why hadn't I smelled it? Was I losing my sense of smell? Was that part of the aging process? I made a mental note to do some reach, but at that moment, I had something more pressing to think about.

I received a call earlier in the day from one of our case management workers in New Orleans. He was in desperate need of fifty training manuals for a workshop he was conducting the next day. I promised to have them delivered, but unless they were in the mailroom in the next thirty minutes, it would not be possible.

Once I had everything packaged, I rushed out the door to the elevator. Within minutes, the mailroom would be closing. I stepped off the elevator a few seconds later and rushed down the hall. As I turned a corner, I felt my left hand tremble. No, not just tremble; it was shaking. I was stressed about meeting the mailroom deadline, but this was a strange sensation. I squeezed my hand into a fist and shook my arm out. By the time I reached the mailroom, the shaking had stopped. I delivered the package and went back to my office. I was convinced the whole episode was a fluke brought on by too much stress - until the next day, when the same thing happened.

I was walking down the hall when I felt the same hand shaking uncontrollably. I raised my arm, and it stopped. I considered myself in reasonably good shape for my age. I got eight hours of sleep a night, went to the gym five days a week and ate a healthy diet; well, not too healthy, but not too bad either. I had been having some nagging neck pain. Perhaps a pinched nerve was at the root of all my problems. When I had a chance, I would schedule an appointment for a check-up. There was no cause for alarm.

The next few weeks passed in a flurry of work and family responsibilities. Kathryn had recently moved into her own apartment, and I had fun helping her decorate. It was an exciting time in her life. Her relationship with Adam was going well, and he was a month away from law-school graduation. He had accepted a job at a firm in New York so that after five long years, he and Kathryn would finally be residents of the same city again.

I still experienced neck pain and hand trembling, but I hadn't yet seen a doctor. I didn't think there was any real cause for alarm. I would schedule a check-up later in the month. Right now, I needed to find a swimsuit.

Two weeks later, Rick and I flew to Florida for a friend's wedding at the Four Seasons resort in Palm Beach. Within hours of arrival, we were settled in beach chairs and sipping frozen daiquiris. It was April, and back in New York, the weather was still cold and gray. Laying in the sun felt glorious, and it took considerable coaxing to get me back to our room in time to change for dinner.

The next morning we woke to a beautiful, cloudless day. The weather was perfect for an outdoor wedding. The ceremony was in the Jewish tradition, and the dark blue of the ocean and sky made a stunning backdrop for the rose-covered chuppah. As our friends pledged their love, everyone clinked champagne glasses and cheered.

I glanced at Rick and felt my heart flood with emotion. Our love was as strong as the day we took our own vows, and he was the one responsible. He had always been the generous and understanding one. He watched over my happiness and well-being as if they were his own.

That evening, we laughed, snapped photos and toasted the newlyweds. A fabulous band entertained us throughout dinner, and we were anxious to hit the dance floor. As soon as the waiters cleared our table, Rick reached for my hand. It was such a familiar gesture, but it made me smile.

I thought we would always be that happy, and that our best days were still ahead, but I was wrong. Seconds later, I learned happiness can be snatched from anyone, at any time, without warning.

The crowd of well-wishers gathered around the bride and groom made it hard to reach the dance floor. When we finally made it, we noticed a group of friends from Nashville dancing nearby and joined them. Rick was all smiles as he twirled me around and gyrated to the beat of the music. What happened next, gripped me with fear bordering on panic. I started to dance, but nothing happened. My legs wouldn't move. I felt as if someone had glued them to the floor. My entire lower body felt stiff and heavy, as if weights were attached to my ankles. Thoughts raced through my mind like lightning. What was happening? Why couldn't I dance? I willed my legs to move, but they wouldn't. Horrified, I used my upper body to sway with the music. I didn't want to alarm anyone. This was a wedding; it was supposed to be a happy time. I smiled and tried to act as if nothing was happening, but inside I was terrified. My brain wasn't communicating with my legs, and at that moment, I suddenly knew all the strange episodes I had recently experienced – my loss of smell, the stiffness in my neck and trembling hand - were all somehow related.

Rick didn't detect what was happening, but when the song ended, I motioned for him to return with me to our table. Oddly, I didn't find it difficult to walk. I encouraged Rick to dance with old friends we seldom got to see while I chatted with our former neighbors from Nashville. Whenever he asked if I'd like to dance, I made up an excuse. He was having fun and too occupied to notice I never left our table again.

When the evening ended, we said goodnight and headed to our room. The elevator was full of wedding guests laughing and talking about how enjoyable the weekend had been. As Rick unlocked the door to our room, he commented on how much fun he had dancing. I chose my words carefully before speaking.

"I couldn't dance."

"Don't be ridiculous. You're a wonderful dancer."

He didn't realize I was referring to my lack of movement. Why should he? I'd spent the entire night hiding it from him.

Being in our room and away from the dance floor helped calm my nerves and made me feel less anxious. I decided not to say anything about the incident to Rick. It would only frighten him, and it probably wasn't as serious as I imagined. When we got home, I would learn more and then let him know. For now, what I needed was for him to hold me and help me forget my fear. Ecclesiastes 3:4 says, "There is a time to weep and a time to laugh, a time to mourn and a time to dance." There would be time for everything one day, but for now, all I wanted was to lay in Rick's arms and pretend nothing had happened.

We flew home the next day, and I tried to put my worry to rest. I convinced myself whatever was wrong was minor. I might need a particular vitamin or a shot of something. Whatever was wrong, it could be fixed. I now realize I was in a state of denial.

On Monday, I arrived at work early and turned on my computer. I opened a search engine, entered all the symptoms I had experienced and pressed enter. The words *Parkinson's disease* were everywhere. It was a mistake. It had to be a mistake. I closed the window on my screen and picked up my mail.

Two days passed before I summoned up enough courage to research Parkinson's disease. I went to the Michael J. Fox Foundation's website and read for hours. From what I learned, Parkinson's disease destroys cells in the brain that control movement. As a result, it can cause limbs to shake, the way may hand had, or become stiff and not move at all, the way my neck and legs did. Some people have difficulty with sleep, memory loss, balance, coordination – and loss of smell. I read that Parkinson's isn't fatal, but it is chronic and progressive, and while many treatments are available, *there is no cure.*

My symptoms were signs of this chronic, degenerative neurological disorder. I knew self-diagnosis could be dangerous, but I was only fooling myself if I pretended there wasn't a chance I had Parkinson's disease. In fact, the more I researched, the more convinced I became it was more than possible; it was probable. Even so, I told no one - not even Rick. Something inside me couldn't accept this outcome. Even as the evidence piled up, I clung to hope it was all a mistake.

At the end of May, we traveled to Charlottesville to celebrate Adam's graduation from law school. The sun beamed, but it was Adam's face that made me smile. The last time I saw him dressed in a cap and gown was on a spring day in 2002 when I snapped a photo of him and Kathryn on Locust Walk at Penn. They were older now and the years of work and study showed on their faces, but they still glowed when they looked at each other and I captured it in my photos that day.

I had just finished speaking with Adam's parents when Kathryn came to me and whispered, "Why is your hand shaking?"

I could hear the fear in her voice.

"It's not," I said.

"Yes it is. Why are you trying to hide it?"

She hesitated before adding, "Mom, you don't have Parkinson's disease do you?"

Her voice was trembling, and I was shocked. Where had she come up with this diagnosis? Had she noticed symptoms I thought I had hidden from her? I couldn't drill her without exposing the truth.

"Of course not. I've been having some problems with my neck, and sometimes I get a spasm in an arm or hand. I may have a pinched nerve."

"Are you sure it's nothing more?"

"Kathryn, if I had Parkinson's disease, I'd tell you."

"No, you wouldn't. You wouldn't tell me until it became absolutely necessary."

I cringed. How would I ever break such devastating news to my daughter?

"Everything is all right. There's no need to worry." I repeated.

When the ceremony ended, I walked back to the car in silence. If Kathryn noticed my hand trembling, it was only a matter of time before Rick and others did. The moment I had been putting off for months had arrived. It was time to share my concerns with Rick. I had done everything possible to avoid this moment. I have a strong will and told myself if I could convince my mind this wasn't happening, then it wouldn't. Once I spoke the name of this disease, shared the secret with anyone or acknowledged it in any way, it would become real. I would lose control of it, and it would exist. I wasn't trying to protect myself. I knew what was happening. I was trying to protect everyone I loved – for as long as I could.

In some ways, this was like trying to protect a sand castle. When the surf attacks your creation, you grab your bucket and start bailing. If you bail fast enough and hard enough, you can keep the castle safe – for a while. You have no illusions. You know the surf will attack again. It's inevitable, but you keep bailing because it's all you can do. You have to protect the castle. You can't just let the tide take it. You love it too much. You watch the waves grow bigger and come in closer. You can't move the castle out of danger, so you lay down in front of it. It's your only hope, but it won't work. The waves will eventually engulf the castle. You'll watch as it's battered by the surf, and you'll stand there telling yourself it's your fault. It's your castle. You should be able to protect it.

On our drive back to New York, I told Rick everything I had experienced in the past few months.

"Whatever is wrong involves my brain, and I'm frightened,"

He reached over and took my hand.

"I know you're scared, but try not to worry. First thing in the morning, call your doctor and make an appointment. We'll take this one step at a time. Remember, whatever it is, we'll face it together."

It was real. There was no going back.

I called the next day and scheduled a consultation with my primary care physician. The night before my appointment, I arrived home from work, grabbed a book and headed for my favorite bench in Central Park. Rick would know where to find me.

At seven o'clock, I looked up and saw him walking towards me. He sat down and put his arm around me.

"What would you like to do tonight?"

I knew he wanted to ease my apprehension, but the situation was too critical to sidestep.

"I don't know what's wrong, but I do know it's serious, and we have to be prepared. I have a feeling this diagnosis will change our lives forever."

"So, what would you like to do tonight?" he repeated.

"I want to walk through the park, have dinner at Café Mozart, and drink lots of wine."

"Sounds good to me. Let's get started."

We held hands and walked to Café Mozart.

The small room where the nurse left me the next day was cold, and the thin gown I was wearing didn't begin to block the chill. I folded my arms across my chest, hugged my body tightly and tried to stay calm. A few minutes later, Dr. Scalia arrived. He was a young doctor and I had been his patient since I first arrived in New York.

"What brings you here today? I've never seen you sick. Patients like you put doctors out of business."

I appreciated his humor and his effort to lessen my anxiety, but nothing could make this situation any easier. I described the symptoms I was experiencing and the event at the wedding. He examined me and posed a number of questions.

I was anxious and finally blurted out, "Can I tell you what I think I have?"

"What do you think you have?" he asked.

"I think I have Parkinson's disease."

He was quiet and studied my face before he spoke.

"I'd be surprised if that's the case. You don't exhibit the level of involvement typically seen in a patient with Parkinson's disease."

I experienced tremendous relief – until I realized he suspected something even more dangerous.

"You have a general weakness on the left side of your body. It concerns me, and I'd like to schedule an MRI for tomorrow morning."

Based on his exam, I knew he suspected a brain tumor might be at the root of my problems. Suddenly, Parkinson's disease didn't seem so bad.

Rick planned to be in D.C. the next day for an overnight conference. He insisted on canceling the trip, but I refused to let him.

"I'm sure I won't learn anything tomorrow. It could be days before I get any results."

In the end, he conceded and agreed to make the trip.

I went to the hospital alone the next morning and signed in at the reception desk. I had never had an MRI, but I had heard the experience described. I was nervous and tried to focus on positive thoughts.

Someone called my name, and I jumped. A nurse led me to the room where the MRI would be performed. The small table I was directed to lay on would soon enter the tube in front of me.

"Keep your eyes shut, and hold your breath when you're told to," the nurse said. "Would you like some earplugs to help with the noise?"

The noise? What noise?

The table approached the machine, and I closed my eyes. I needed to focus on something else – something to transport my mind from this awful place. I decided to visualize my apartment. I would walk through one room at a time and concentrate on each object in it.

A sound similar to bashing pots and pans together suddenly filled the silence. It was deafening. I closed my eyes tighter and focused on walking through my apartment. The MRI was only supposed to last for twenty minutes, but it seemed to go on much longer. When it was over, I felt like I was being pulled from the belly of a monster.

I was told to get dressed and someone would escort me to my neurologist's office. What neurologist? I didn't have a neurologist. Apparently, I did now.

"I've looked at the results of your MRI," he said, "and everything looks fine. There is a small spot on the frontal lobe of the brain, but it doesn't appear to amount to anything. It might be the result of a fall sometime in your past. Regardless, it's of no concern," he said.

Great news, but what about my symptoms?

"I'd like to perform a series of tests that will help me diagnose the problems you're having. If you'll follow me down the hall, we'll begin."

First, I walked back and forth. Next, I sat down and got up, shut my eyes and touched my nose, tapped my feet fast then faster, made fists and in due course, fell backwards into his arms. I wondered about the point of these ridiculous activities. None of them caused me any trouble. We returned to his office, and he sat down at his desk and motioned for me to take a seat.

"I'm sorry to have to tell you this, but you're in the beginning stages of Parkinson's disease. It's a degenerative disease of the central nervous system, and it's caused by the death of cells producing dopamine in the brain. The most common symptoms are movement related. For example, shaking, rigidity, slowness of movement, difficulty walking and problems with balance. As the disease progresses, it is not uncommon to experience emotional problems or difficulty thinking. The cause is unknown, and there is no cure. There are, however, medications that help ease the symptoms, and I can prescribe them for you today. Do you have any questions?"

Questions? I couldn't think of questions. I had just lost my last ounce of hope.

"Can you treat this, or do I need to see a specialist?" I asked.

"I can treat it."

"All right."

"I'll have my nurse come in to go over your medications. Goodbye and good luck to you."

He shook my hand and left the room.

Good luck? What an odd thing to say. I didn't need good luck. I was going to be all right – I had to be all right. I would *make* myself be all right.

I decided to walk the thirty blocks back to our apartment; I needed fresh air, sunlight and time to think. If I hadn't insisted on Rick going to DC, he would be here now. I didn't want to tell him my diagnosis over the phone, but I was desperate to talk with someone.

I phoned Christ Church, but my ministers were attending a conference out-of-town and would not be back for several days. I resisted involving Kathryn because she and Adam were leaving on a trip to Europe soon. Their relationship seemed stronger than ever, and I refused to taint their trip with this disturbing news.

By the time I reached home, I knew to whom I could speak. I reached for the phone and dialed Johnny.

"You've handled a lot of stressful situations in your life, and you'll handle this one. You're strong, and you're going to be all right," he said.

My little brother was always there for me when I needed him.

The phone rang not long after we hung up. It was Rick, who wanted to know how things went at the hospital.

"Everything went fine."

"Did you get any results?"

"Yes, but let's wait until you get back to talk about them."

I thought the silence would last forever.

"Are you sure?"

"I'm sure."

"All right. I'll be home as soon as I can get away tomorrow. In the meantime, if you need anything, promise me you'll call."

"I will."

"I love you."

I hung up, and for the first time that day, I cried.

It was the longest night of my life. Sleep was impossible. I tossed and turned until half the covers ended up on the floor. I cried and swore, made threats and promises. Prayed, bargained and even begged. I felt anger, grief and fear. Parkinson's disease would ravish my body and mind until one day I wouldn't recognize myself. Worst of all, it would wreak havoc on the lives of everyone I loved, and I couldn't stop it from happening. The sense of powerlessness I felt was devastating.

By the time the first streak of light hit the window, I was exhausted and drained of emotion. It was the darkest, most intense night of my life, and although I hadn't won the battle, I had faced the enemy. I endured the grief, said goodbye to myself and prepared to begin a journey down an unfamiliar road.

I didn't blame God, and I hope I never do, but anything is possible. I can sympathize with those who turn away from God when grief overwhelms them, but my experiences shape what I believe, and my experience tells me that God mourns with me. I asked God for courage to let this disease bring out the best in me and not the worst. I prayed to be of use to others and not a burden. I was determined to look for the best in each day and not waste valuable time on self-pity.

My requests had nothing to do with self-righteousness. I was being practical. Anger and resentment breed misery, and I didn't want their company on my new road. My load was heavy enough without the burden of hauling them around. I was searching for ways to bring joy back into my life. I didn't want this disease, but it wasn't my choice. My only choice was whether I let it define my life, and I was determined it would not.

Rick arrived home late the next evening. When the door of the apartment opened, he dropped his bags and hugged me against his chest. We had discussed my symptoms often during the past week and I had shared my suspicions with him. Even so, I don't think he was prepared.

"I can't imagine how you must feel, but we'll get through this together. I love you, and I'll always be here for you."

The first time he made that pledge, we were a couple of teenagers starting out life together. He had spent the past thirty years proving I could trust him, and I did. As we stood there with our arms around each other, I think I loved him more at that moment than at any other time in my life.

When Kathryn returned from Europe, I shared the news with her. A special bond exists between us, and not surprisingly, her first response was to cry.

"You don't deserve this," she said.

"No one does. This isn't a punishment. It's a disease - a disease that's studied every day. There's plenty of reason for hope."

I didn't know if there was hope or not, but it was important for her to believe there was.

I thought I would feel better once I began my medications, but instead I grew worse. I was still seeing the neurologist who diagnosed my condition, but his strategy seemed to change from one office visit to the next. Nothing he suggested seemed to help. After three months of treatment, my balance was worse, and I felt so fatigued I could barely make it through work without falling asleep.

"Nancy?"

I opened my eyes and saw Sam Dixon, the head of UMCOR, standing next to my desk.

"I'm sorry, Sam. I must have dozed off."

"Are you all right? You look tired."

"Actually, if you have a moment, there's something we need to discuss."

We went to his office, and I told him about my diagnosis. He proposed a reduced work schedule until I felt better. I agreed and was thankful for his support.

I cut back on my hours at work but worried what my co-workers must think. Sam was the only person who knew I had Parkinson's disease. I wish I could say courage kept me silent, that I was brave and didn't want to burden others, but it was fear that kept me from speaking out. I was afraid of losing my identity, being marginalized and pitied. I was convinced that once I was labeled with Parkinson's disease, I would cease to be me. This silence came at a high cost. The physical effort required to maintain the appearance of wellness drove me to an overwhelming state of fatigue. I was in bed by six o'clock every night.

My colleague and friend, Clint Rhabb, stopped by my desk one morning to visit. Clint was the director of United Methodist Volunteers in Mission for The United Methodist Church. He traveled extensively throughout the U.S. and abroad organizing members of the church to serve where needs are greatest. We were usually the first to arrive at work and often shared our first cup of coffee together. I always looked forward to our conversations, but not that day. I hadn't rested well the night before, and maneuvering the subway had been treacherous. I had fallen asleep and missed my stop. It was only eight o'clock, but I was already feeling tired.

Clint stood at the corner of my desk smiling and asked how I was doing. I tried to think of a response to hide my condition, but I was too tired to fight that battle any longer. My throat tightened, and I fought back the tears filling my eyes.

"Things aren't going very well right now. I was just diagnosed with Parkinson's disease."

Clint looked in my eyes for a moment, took a sip of coffee and then shrugged his shoulders.

"Well, what the heck? We all have something."

I was so appalled my mouth dropped open. Didn't he understand what I just said? How could he be so flippant and insensitive? Then it happened. The corners of his mouth turned up, and a smile spread across his face. The next moment we both found ourselves laughing aloud. Clint loved to joke, and he knew from the forlorn expression on my face laughter was exactly what I needed.

"You should have seen the look on your face. You were mortified," he said. Clint's response was perfect. Parkinson's disease? So what? We all have something.

I had spent weeks trying to hide my illness, but Clint's reaction helped me overcome the fear of having my diagnosis become public. Buried within his words was the affirmation I needed to hear: I was different, but I was still me. From that moment on, it was easier to talk about Parkinson's disease.

I worried about how people would react to my diagnosis, but in most cases, I found my own attitude set the tenor for their response. I was grateful for Clint's support. He came along at precisely the right moment, with just the right words. Sadly, within a few short months, he would be in much greater need than me and I could do nothing to help.

In January 2010, Clint and Sam were in Port-au-Prince working on ways to expand health care in Haiti when a magnitude seven earthquake tore the city apart. Within seconds, they were trapped beneath the rubble of the Hotel Montana. A French rescue team found them fifty-five hours later, but they were barely alive. Clint was evacuated to a hospital in Florida but died shortly thereafter from injuries he suffered during the earthquake. Sam never made it out of the ruins. He succumbed to heart failure as he was being rescued.

Their tragic deaths taught me how fragile and unpredictable life can be. Clint was right. *We all have something.* His death is a sad and constant reminder that *my* something could be a whole lot worse.

It was a relief to make my diagnosis known, but I continued to lose ground. On my worst days, I was barely able to get out of bed, walk without tripping or do simple task like the laundry or making the bed. I made up excuses to keep Kathryn away from our apartment. I didn't know which would be harder for her – to be left out of my battle or to become a part of it. In the end, I chose to shield her.

I was sitting at my desk on a Friday morning when I began to shake – not just my hand but also my entire body. It was less like a tremor than an intense shiver. I phoned my neurologist who instructed me to go home immediately and get in bed. He believed my body was reacting to another change in my medications. I went home and crawled into bed.

The next three days were a living hell. My body shook so violently I could barely eat, sleep or get out of bed. I dragged myself to the bathroom on my hands and knees and struggled to dial the phone to call in sick at the office.

Rick was out-of-town, as were Kathryn and Adam. I had friends I could call, but I couldn't stand to think of anyone seeing me in such a dreadful state. When my neurologist finally returned my frantic calls, he told me to increase my medications.

"Don't expect a miracle," he warned. "It could be several days before you notice a difference."

Several days? I wasn't sure I could survive another six hours. I decided to phone my friend Camille. She was a few years older than Kathryn was and had been our neighbor in Tennessee for many years. She was now Dr. Camille Vaughan, an eminent geriatric and gerontology physician at Emory University. With trembling hands, I dialed her number.

The first thing she did was evaluate my current state to determine if I needed to go to the hospital. She would prefer I did, but I resisted. She listened to a detailed list of my medications and admitted to being confused over some of the choices my neurologist had made.

"Why aren't you going to Columbia for treatment?" she asked. "They have one of the premier centers for movement disorders in the country, and it's right there in New York!"

She gave me a list of doctors at Columbia University Medical Center and urged me to make an appointment immediately.

"Getting the right treatment in the early stages of the disease can make a huge difference in the long run," she insisted.

Then, as if sensing my hesitancy, she added, "But don't just do this for you. Do it for Rick and Kathryn."

Her words were still echoing in my mind four days later as I sat in a waiting room outside the office of famed neurologist Dr. Cheryl Waters, M.D. She is the Chief of Clinical Practice and Services at Columbia's Division of Movement Disorders and one of the country's leading specialists in the treatment of Parkinson's disease.

I was trying to stay positive, but it wasn't easy. Across from me sat a man who looked to be in his sixties. His right hand was shaking so badly he could barely hold the magazine he was trying to read. Two seats away, an older woman with white hair was slumped so low in her wheelchair that I was afraid she might fall out. Another man in a wheelchair sat next to his wife, who occasionally reached up to wipe his mouth with a handkerchief. My future was in front of my eyes, and it was frightening.

A nurse called my name and escorted me to an exam room. Dr. Waters was seated at a small desk in the corner, reading my file. She had cropped black hair and a direct gaze. She introduced herself then asked abruptly,

"Did you come here alone today?"

"Yes."

"How did you get here?"

"I took the subway."

"The subway?" She looked alarmed. "You're in no condition to be on the subway. Do you have money for a cab?"

"Yes, but I'd prefer not take one unless it's absolutely necessary."

Dr. Waters closed the file she had been reading and stared at me.

"Necessary?" she said. "It could be a matter of life or death. If you're taking all of the medications listed in this file, there are enough narcotics in you to put a horse to sleep. I'm surprised you can even walk."

Tears welled in my eyes, and without taking her eyes off my face, Dr. Waters reached over and handed me some tissues.

"Your body is like a house that was poorly renovated," she continued. "We need to go back in, tear out a lot of things and rebuild."

Columbia University's Division of Movement Disorders was at the forefront of Parkinson's research and Dr. Waters had conducted numerous studies on optimal treatment protocols. The strategy she recommended for me would take time to implement. First, I would need to withdraw from my current medications.

"It may take several months to develop a specific protocol for you, but when we're finished, you're going to feel a lot better," she said.

I don't recall how long I cried, but I went through a lot more than my initial handful of tissues. In truth, I hadn't expected to improve. I was struggling to accept things as they were.

What ensued was nothing short of a miracle - at least to me. Under the skillful care of Dr. Waters, within a month my energy level increased, my mobility improved, and I regained my sense of balance. I felt happier than I had in months. Week by week I improved and began adding back activities I thought I would never enjoy again. I went for walks in the park, attended social events and even made it through an entire movie without falling asleep.

I had no illusions or false expectations. When Dr. Waters prescribed the medication that helped get me to this point, she did so with the honesty and forthrightness for which I came to admire her.

"This medication should give you five to six good years. After that, it will become less effective, and you'll experience side effects, which can be difficult to manage."

Five to six good years sounded like an eternity to someone who had given up hope of ever experiencing another ordinary day – a day when I laughed, loved and knew what it meant to be happy. She gave me back my life and my future. How do you thank someone for a gift like that?

Just when I thought nothing could make me happier, something did. Adam asked to come over one afternoon without Kathryn.

"I suppose you know why I'm here," he said.

It was a Saturday afternoon, and unless I was mistaken, he was here to tell us he planned to propose. Otherwise, he would be out having fun.

We were delighted. Rick and I had great affection for Adam and knew he would be a fine husband to Kathryn. He planned to surprise her with a ring when they visited Philly at the end of the month.

A wedding! We were having a wedding. A wedding in New York City? How would we ever pull it off?

PANTY HOSE

35

It was a bright and windy morning in June, and the legendary Cosmopolitan Club had never looked prettier. Downstairs in the Grand Ballroom, thirty tables were adorned with white orchids, tapered candles and sparkling crystal.

The bride and groom's cupcake tower had been delivered hours ago, and twenty cases of champagne were being chilled. An eight-piece band was doing a final sound check, and the photographer was meeting us in twenty minutes. Ten months of painstaking planning were about to culminate in my daughter's dream wedding, and what was I doing? I was flopped across the bed, sobbing over a pair of panty hose or, to be exact, the lack of them.

"How could I forget to buy panty hose for my own daughter's wedding?" I wailed to Rick.

"I thought you were wearing sandals."

"I am, but what if I change my mind and need panty hose?"

"Do you want me to walk over to Duane Reed and buy you a pair?"

"No, it's too late. The photographer will be here any minute. I'll just have to make do without them."

I turned my back to Rick and cried into my pillow. He sat down and massaged my back.

"This isn't about panty hose," he said.

"What do you mean?"

"Don't you see what's happening? You're having a meltdown. You put your heart and soul into this wedding, and now that it's here, you're afraid something will go wrong. But, it won't. We have everything covered. Michelle is doing a great job."

When Rick first suggested I hire someone to help me the day of the wedding, I refused and said I could handle everything myself. Thankfully, his common sense prevailed over my stubborn pride. He knew if I tried to oversee everything on my own, I wouldn't last through the wedding, much less the evening. I relented, hired my colleague Michelle and placed everything in her capable hands.

Rick was also right about the panty hose. I hadn't worn hose in at least five years. Why would I need them now? I washed my face and reapplied my make-up. It was time to meet the photographer.

Thoughts of hosting a wedding in Manhattan had initially terrified me. I couldn't imagine navigating through the process. However, much to my surprise, everything fell in place with astonishing ease. When my friend Carolyn, who was serving as president of the Cosmopolitan Club, learned of Kathryn's engagement, she generously offered to sponsor the wedding at the Club. In addition to its beautiful ballroom, the Club also serves as a boutique hotel for members and their guests. We not only had accommodations for the bride and groom but also for our families. Best of all, Christ Church, where the wedding ceremony would take place, was only six blocks away.

Later that evening, as Rick walked Kathryn down the aisle of our church, I looked at Adam and saw an expression on his face that will live in my memory forever. His eyes were focused on Kathryn, and I don't believe he was aware of anyone else in the church. The two of them stood with Reverend Bauman, pledging their love to each other, and I knew in my mind's eye, they would never grow old. To me, they would always be the two young people I watched gaze into each other's eyes that day.

Following the ceremony, we arranged for a bagpiper to lead guests from the church to the Cosmopolitan Club. Kathryn and Adam, hand in hand, led the parade as well-wishers in cars, cabs and apartments cheered, waved and took pictures.

Later that night, as our guests finished dinner and waiters scurried to refill wine glasses, I paused for a moment to savor the day. Our families, as well as friends from every chapter of our lives, had traveled to New York to be with us. Their outpouring of love was over-whelming.

I glanced across the ballroom and noticed Johnny standing next to the band. I was grateful to him for taking care of our mother, now eighty-five, and bringing her to the wedding. Several weeks earlier, I phoned and informed her of my diagnosis. I couldn't risk her learning of it during her visit. The last thing I wanted was for her to be blind-sided. She took the news with her usual positive outlook.

"I don't want you to worry. You're going to be just fine," she said.

Hearing it from her almost convinced me it was true.

This was Johnny's first trip to New York. I regretted not having time to show him around the city, but I did have a surprise for him.

"Follow me," I whispered in his ear.

We left the ballroom and took the elevator to the top floor. When the door opened, we stepped into a dark room.

"Do you know where we're going?" he asked.

"Don't you trust me?" I laughed.

We made our way to a set of doors on the opposite side of the room. I unlocked them and then turned to Johnny.

"This is the surprise I've been waiting to show you."

I stepped out onto a balcony, and Johnny followed close behind.

"This is my city, and I wanted to show it to you."

It was dark, and the trillion lights that give New York its glitz never shown brighter. It was several minutes before Johnny spoke.

"It's a big place."

"It doesn't seem as big once you get used to it."

"I'm not sure I could ever get used to this."

I smiled because I knew the last thing he would ever want was to live in a place like New York. Johnny never married and still lives in our hometown, not far from my mother and Linda. He built a house for himself years ago that sits in the middle of the woods across from rolling farmland. He doesn't care for large cities. He prefers to live a simple life and to surround himself with the delights of nature. He is a ferocious reader, loves classical music, fishing and gardening. He spends much of his day in solitude, but a peaceful lifestyle suits him well.

Linda and her family were downstairs enjoying the dance floor. She was expecting her first grandchild soon. Our busy schedules prevent us from speaking often, but when we do, our conversations are always laced with love and understanding. She still struggles with issues concerning our father, and I think a part of her always will.

My mother looked lovely as Rick escorted her down the aisle during the ceremony. She was now relishing in the compliments being paid to her by our friends. My only regret was the lack of time we would have together. With each move Rick and I made, the miles between my mother and I increased. I am no longer the person she turns to for support. Linda and Johnny now fill that role. My part is smaller but not shallower. It's not unusual for my mother to write me a note for no reason other than to say she loves me.

Earlier in the evening, I was speaking with my niece's husband, Rob, when he mentioned a recent visit Linda and my mother made to his home.

In his usual playful way, he had asked my mother what Linda was like as a teenager.

"Your mother said Linda wasn't a problem, but she could fill a book with *your* escapades."

I suppose there are some things a mother never forgets. Regardless, I'm glad I beat her to sharing my secrets. There's no telling what she might have revealed.

"I suppose I better get back downstairs," I said to Johnny. "Rick will be wondering what happened to me."

We stood on the balcony a few more minutes, neither of us trying to fill the quiet. Silence is only uncomfortable when people aren't at peace with each other.

I went to bed late that night and slept longer than I intended. I rushed to get downstairs the next morning before Kathryn and Adam left for their honeymoon. I had forgotten to plan a proper send-off, and they would be leaving any minute.

Family members staying at the Club were beginning to gather along the front walk to say goodbye to the newlyweds. I scanned the room, frantically searching for something I could use to make their departure special. My eyes landed on some floral arrangements from the reception. I quickly pulled off dozens of blossoms and distributed them to everyone outside.

Seconds later, Kathryn and Adam came out the front door and were showered with miniature orchids. They gave me a quick kiss and then hurried off in a cab to meet their plane.

It was a joyful goodbye but still a goodbye, and I stood on the sidewalk looking down 66th Street long after their car disappeared. By the time

I turned toward the Club, everyone was gone. The petals scattered on the sidewalk were the only evidence of our gathering, and in a few hours, even they would disappear. I knew Kathryn would be a wonderful wife, and maybe someday a mother, but it was hard to imagine her being either. It was impossible to think of her as anyone other than my daughter.

I inhaled deeply and looked up at the clear blue sky. It was a beautiful day for our guests to spend in the city. I wanted to go back to bed, but I knew it would take Rick and I most of the day to haul everything back to our apartment.

I hadn't seen Rick all morning and wondered if he made it downstairs for the send-off. I went inside and found him in the library surrounded by three dozen arrangements of orchids and twisted willow branches.

"Are all of these going to our apartment?" he asked.

"Not unless you want to spend the next week feeling like we live in a mortuary."

He looked relieved.

"I didn't see you outside," I said.

"I was there, but as soon as Kathryn and Adam left, I came inside and started packing."

"She's gone, you know. It's not like in the past when she'd come back. This time it's for good."

"I know, but I'm still here. That means something doesn't it?"

He put his arms around my waist, and I lay my head against his chest.

"It means you kept your promise."

"What promise?"

"You said I could trust you, that you wouldn't let me down, and you wouldn't leave."

"When did I say that?"

"A long time ago."

"Did you believe me when I said it?"

"For some reason, I did."

"You still can. Nothing has changed."

I smiled and thought of all the things that had changed.

AFTERWORD

I began this memoir four years ago after moving from Manhattan to the coast of North Carolina. It was a necessary move, but not one I initially embraced.

The recession began in late 2007 and seemed to hit New York overnight. UMCOR responded by cutting forty-five positions, and my job was lost to someone with senior status. Walking away was heart wrenching. Nine months later, after becoming frustrated with the senior leadership at Pace, Rick accepted a position at the University of North Carolina Wilmington, and we headed south.

My morning rush no longer involves hoofing it to the subway, but rather watching pelicans charge into the ocean in hopes of capturing breakfast. If they do, no one will stop to take a picture. Unlike the hawk on Broadway, their presence is a common sight along this stretch of beach.

Writing this book led me on a journey past the highs, the lows and the in-betweens of my life. What did I discover? Happiness necessitates living life in the moment – without worry about the future, without grief or bitterness over the past. Simple pleasures – a walk along the beach, a loved one's hand in mine, they are the only things worth cherishing – worth remembering.

"Come, Gigi," shouts the little golden haired boy ahead of me on the beach. My grandson wants me to pick up my pace and doesn't understand why I can't, but he will someday. I catch up with him, and we start a sandcastle.

"Gigi, tell story," he says.

And, so I do.

"Once upon a time, Gigi and Pops were on their way to meet the Queen of Sweden, but the traffic was very bad . . ."

AUTHOR'S NOTE

I wrote this book from memory, personal interviews and family research. Certain names and identifying characteristics were changed to preserve anonymity.

ACKNOWLEDGMENTS

Writing a book is work, and the more you care about the story, the harder you'll work to create something others will want to read. I choose to be a writer, but if given the choice, I doubt my incredibly patient husband, Rick, would choose to be a writer's spouse. He has my gratitude for giving up so much of our time together. Thank you, my darling, for all the dinners you cooked, the laundry you did, and most of all for taking my work seriously and listening to me read this manuscript hundreds of times while pretending to be interested.

I am indebted to my editor and writing partner, Laura Warner, who kept me motivated during this process by inspiring me with her own writing. I dream of being half the writer she is.

I am profoundly grateful to my daughter, Kathryn Whitfield, who poured over this manuscript for years helping me turn it into something special. Thank you, Kathryn, for sharing your time so generously.

My heartfelt thanks to Dr. Cheryl Waters, at Columbia University, and Dr. Burton Scott, at Duke, for patiently listening to my concerns and rescuing me from the despair of Parkinson's disease.

Prior to the publication of this book, I underwent deep brain stimulation (DBS) at Stanford University Health System. The results have been nothing short of amazing. I wish to thank everyone who helped create this miracle of medicine for me, especially Dr. Casey Halpern, Dr. Jaimie Henderson, Dr. Helen Bronte-Stewart, and Dr. James Barrese.

My appreciation to Joan Ross Sorkin, Jo Ann Mathews, Marty Pedigo, Tina Seamon, Ann Pollack, Judy Hanna, Mary Lee Brown and Pilar Queen for your honest and helpful critiques. In addition, I wish to thank my family and friends for your encouragement through the many years it took to complete this book, and for not balking at all the times you were coerced into listening to parts of it. Please know that your names are written across my heart.

Lastly, to my mother, in her nineties now, who never fails to ask me, "What about your book?" Much of this story is about her own life and the struggles of trying to singlehandedly raise three children during the 50's and 60's. Mom, you always were, and always will be, my inspiration.